Get Set for Religious Studies

Get Set for Religious Studies

Dominic Corrywright and Peggy Morgan

Edinburgh University Press

© Dominic Corrywright and Peggy Morgan, 2006

Edinburgh University Press Ltd
22 George Square, Edinburgh

Typeset in Sabon
by Servis Filmsetting Ltd, Manchester, and
printed and bound in Great Britain by
MPG Books Ltd, Bodmin, Cornwall

A CIP record for this book is available from the British Library

ISBN-10 0 7486 2032 X (paperback)
ISBN-13 978 0 7486 2032 6 (paperback)

CONTENTS

ACKNOWLEDGEMENTS

The authors wish to acknowledge permission given by West-minster Institute of Education, Oxford Brookes University for adaptation of some material originally written for their distance-learning programmes in Theology and Religious Studies.

PART I
Religion and the Study of Religions

PART I   INTRODUCTION

The study of religions could not be more relevant for our understanding of the world and localities in which we live. It is important for understanding politics, practices and cultures, whether or not we are ourselves religious. Living a religious life involves much more than what people believe. It involves their preferred food and dress; their deep roots in particular geographical places and nations; the celebration of festivals; what people believe about life after death; the way they respond to suffering and how this affects hospice care; how they educate their children; the jobs they choose to do; how they use their income; how members of extended families relate to each other, gender roles and relationships between men and women.

After your degree, whether you work in the health services, leisure industries, education, the Foreign Office, legal professions, police force or for a charity, have family members of a variety of traditions or just wish to live in an informed way with your Hindu, Jewish, Muslim and all other neighbours, understanding people's religious orientations and practices is both interesting and important. Of course, this book cannot give you all the facts you need to know about the above, and you may have learned a great deal already. But it does introduce you to a field, the study of which at university level will lay the foundations for being able to access even more information of both a practical and a theoretical kind. It will also lead you to ask all sorts of practical and theoretical questions, and asking questions is the beginning of the kind of exploration which being an undergraduate involves.

Against the backdrop outlined above, this book serves three main purposes. The primary purpose is to introduce you to what is involved in the academic study of religions or religious studies at university undergraduate level. It focuses on religious traditions, some key contemporary issues and on ways of studying or approaching the material (perspectives), which includes mentioning the work of many classical and contemporary scholars working in the field. Because the field is very dynamic, new issues and perspectives are always emerging and being emphasised, so we have not been exhaustive. No author at any one time can cover every approach in a subject with such a rich history and growing contemporary research. Even while this book is going through the process of printing, new volumes of ideas, information and analyses will be on the shelves.

The term field is used rather than discipline, as the study of religions draws on insights and methods from a variety of disciplines, which makes it one of the most varied fields of study that can be undertaken. Whether you are interested in psychology, philosophical issues, sociology, history, ethics, human cultures or language-based study of texts, there is something here for you. One fact that it is important for you to realise is that it is not essential for you to be doing or to have done an AS or A2 level in religious studies to apply for a religious studies course at university. You can begin to work in this field at undergraduate level and departments will be interested in your application on the basis of your lively interest in the study of religions and in your achievements in the subjects on which you have been working. Note that university prospectuses may use the name religious studies, study of religions, theology or even divinity (see Part II Chapter 3), but the most important thing is the syllabus that is offered and whether you will be able to take the kind of courses that are really interesting to you within the degree. Reading this book should give you ideas for relevant questions which you can raise in relation to prospectuses and on any open day or interview to which you are invited.

Secondly, if you are taking advanced level religious studies, reading sections of this book might be useful for your current study and understanding of what the term religion means. It also gives information and ideas about particular religions and how they are studied. These ideas may well extend, or even be different in their approach from the notes and text books with which you have been working. Any differences are intended to make you think. The following chapters also contain background details and information on many key areas that you might not be able to find so conveniently elsewhere.

Thirdly, if you do go on to a university course in the field, you might well find this a useful source book for the first term or semester. Each section has a bibliography of more advanced texts in the area and there is also a useful glossary of terms at the back and an index for you to search for material on a particular topic. You will notice as you progress in your studies which new areas are being opened up and what the issues will be for the future. If you go on to do postgraduate work after an initial degree you will be able to add original work to the field, perhaps in the study of the many *diaspora* communities there are now in all parts of the UK and in other parts of the world; researching the impact of the world wide web on understanding religions; investigating what members of one or more religious traditions have to say on issues such as cloning or euthanasia, or in translating and writing a commentary on a sacred text.

The next chapter begins by asking one of the most basic, but still hotly debated questions in the field. What do we mean by religion? Before you read it, jot down your own initial definition and that of a friend or family member and compare your ideas to those we have presented.

BIBLIOGRAPHY

Cole, W. Owen and Peggy Morgan (2000), *Six Religions in The Twenty First Century*, Cheltenham: Stanley Thornes.

Hinnells, John R. (ed.) [1998] (2nd ed. 2000), *The New Penguin Handbook of Living Religions*, London: Penguin Books.

Morgan, Peggy and Clive Lawton (eds) [1996] (2nd ed. 2006), *Ethical Issues in Six Religious Traditions*, Edinburgh: Edinburgh University Press.

Nesbitt, Eleanor (2004), *Intercultural Education*, Brighton: Sussex Academic Press.

Weller, Paul (ed.) (2001), *Religions in UK: A Directory*, Derby: University of Derby.

Woodward, Peter with Riadh El-Droubie and Cherry Gould (eds) (1998), *Festivals in World Religions*, Norwich: Religious and Moral Education Press.

1. DESCRIBING AND DEFINING RELIGION

1. INTRODUCTION

Questions of definition can seem dry at first, but with a word that we use as often as 'religion' everyone has their views and associations, so discussion is usually lively. Some people are sympathetic towards religion and some hostile. An interesting preliminary to the discussion that follows, which we suggested in the Introduction, might be to jot down your own attempt at a definition and ask some other people you know of different ages and if possible from a variety of religious or non-religious backgrounds to give you their ideas. You will find it interesting to see, as this section develops, how the definitions you have collected relate to the points made by a variety of scholars. John Bowker remarks in his Introduction to the *Oxford Dictionary of World Religions* that 'a strange thing about religion is that we all know what it is until someone asks us to tell them' (Bowker, 1997: xv). He then lists some key definitions from thinkers of varied backgrounds, many of whom are important for the variety of approaches we shall be considering in Part II.

For people from a Christian or post-Christian background, the term 'religion' may first and foremost be a matter of what people believe and in particular what they believe about God. But those who are Jewish, Muslim, Hindu or Sikh, or who study these traditions, may prefer to emphasise that they are ways of life and that religion is an unsympathetic term if it is associated primarily with belief. For them religion is first and foremost a matter of what you do, not what you think. There is an emphasis on community, what you eat, what you wear, who and how you marry and how you treat your elders. In India it is *orthopraxy* (doing the right thing) not orthodoxy (believing the right thing) which defines who you are and whether your religious community will accept you. This has been true for most societies except in the secular-biased Western world since the eighteenth century *Enlightenment*. Whether we like it or not, it would be blind not to admit that for most people religion is still first and foremost an identity, a label, a badge of allegiance to a group: *Protestant* and *Roman Catholic* in Ulster; Hindu and Sikh in the Punjab; *Sunni* and *Shi'a* in Iraq; Jewish Israeli or Muslim Palestinian. People claim these identities or have them forced upon them to show whose side they are on. In this sense religion cannot be separated from politics, or indeed from racism, for these badges are used in struggles for power, resources and survival. On the issue of religion as an institutional reality or a personal committment, Wilfred Cantwell Smith (1916–2000 CE) suggested in *The Meaning and End of Religion* (1978) that we should distinguish between cumulative traditions to which we give the names Christianity, Sikhism and so on, and the faith of individual men and women.

As we go on to look at various scholars' suggestions for ways of defining and describing religion and religions, you will find that some agree and some disagree with the ideas you have collected. By the end of this section your own understanding will probably have changed, and that is a journey which will continue with further study. You may also notice that some people prefer the term *spirituality* to the term religion, suggesting that religions are about institutions and external rituals, established ways of believing and what is official, enshrined in tradition and regulated by authority and the commandments of sacred texts, what is formal, dogmatic and often male-dominated. *Spirituality*, on the other hand, is linked with what people discover and own personally, that which is interior or present in more than one religion. It is their own experience of relationship with the sacred, accompanied by a sense of wisdom and action on issues of the environment and justice, which derives from such experience (see Heelas in Woodhead *et al.*, 2002: 358).

2. MAKING MODELS OF RELIGION

Many thinkers, in different ways, want to embrace the distinctions between belief and practice mentioned above. Richard Gombrich, who has worked extensively on Buddhism and Hinduism, describes three dimensions of religion, which he sees as dimensions of all human experience. These are **action, belief** and **emotion** and he says that world religions take account of all three but emphasise them differently. Religions can be about the search for material benefits: wealth, fertility and medical cures, or a way of acting in society and conforming to the customs of a group as well as the personal quest for ultimate meaning.

One of the most original and influential models for understanding what the word 'religion' embraces is that described by Ninian Smart (1927–2001 CE) in many of his books. He emphasises that religion is a complex phenomenon with many dimensions. When he originally suggested his model in the late 1960s, he listed six dimensions, but by the 1990s, these had increased to seven and even nine. This shows that he did not think of the model as static and watertight but as a helpful and flexible way to understand the family resemblances between the religions we encounter and study. Smart gave the dimensions various names to reduce any sense of rigidity in what he is describing. His model has been used as a framework for Damien Keown's book *Buddhism: A Very Short Introduction*, which shows that it is successful when applied to a religion where a definition such as 'belief in God or gods' is inappropriate.

Smart suggests that the dimensions of any religion are related organically. His image is that of the organs of the body, none of which function on their own if you remove them from their relationships with the other parts, from the network of the body as a whole. They are interlinked, interactive and interdependent.

Smart also affirms the relevance of studying religions in three ways. Firstly, study is necessary for understanding the story, what some would call the history, of humankind's various experiments in living. Secondly, it is needed to grasp the politics and cultural identities of the world in which we live and thirdly, it may help us when we are forming our own coherent and emotionally satisfying picture of reality. He also says that in undertaking a voyage into the world's religions we should not define religion too narrowly and that it is important for us to recognise that secular ideologies such as humanism are part of the story of human worldviews. It is artificial to divide them too sharply from religions, partly because they sometimes function in society like religions, and partly because the distinction between religion and secular beliefs and practices is a modern Western one and does not represent the way in which people from other cultures think. Furthermore, he emphasises that to understand religious and secular worldviews and their practical meaning we have to use imagination. We have to enter into the lives of those for whom such ideas and actions are important. He often quoted the proverb from the *indigenous* peoples of North America: 'Never judge a person until you have walked a mile in their moccasins'.

Smart points out that the voyage of understanding he is advocating begins in our own diverse neighbourhoods and takes into account the great varieties of Christianities that are there as well as varieties of other religions. Within these, mixed-faith marriages, personal encounters and pilgrimages of faith may cause people to cross the external divisions of religious labels and see themselves as religiously bilingual. Some Christians may feel closer to some Buddhists than to very differently oriented members of their own religious tradition, for example.

Smart presents seven key but different aspects or dimensions of religion. These are:

The Practical or Ritual Dimension

This dimension includes worship, preaching, the use of sacraments and rites of passage, prayers and sacrifices. These aspects of religion are more important for some religious people than others, even within any one religion. Some Christians, for example the members of the Society of Friends (*Quakers*), minimise ritual, whilst members of the *Eastern Orthodox* traditions are involved in a very considerable ritual life. *Sufis* within Islam may challenge external rituals and emphasise the pilgrimage to God within the heart, whilst to other Muslims the *Hajj* (pilgrimage) remains an essential physical journey to be made once in a lifetime.

The Experiential and Emotional Dimension

Experience has been seminal in the origins and maintenance of religious life. Examples of this are the experience of the *Buddha* under the Bodhi Tree, Muhammad on Mount Hira, Moses at the Burning Bush and the Conversion of St Paul. For the ordinary member of a religious tradition, rituals without this experiential dimension become empty and dry. Religious life is full of the language of sacred awe, calm peace, the outpouring of love, gratitude, hope and dynamism for change.

The Narrative or Mythic Dimension

Experience is often channelled or stimulated both by rituals and the sacred stories (*myths*) of religions. All faiths hand down stories. Some of them are historical, some creation myths beyond the dawn of time, some the stories of key figures such as Moses or the *Buddha* or Muhammad or Jesus, some parables. What is important in these stories is the understandings of reality that they convey and they are formed into the sacred scriptures of the traditions. These are usually the source for the ritual dimension: for example the Jewish Passover *Seder* is rooted in the story of the Exodus from Egypt.

The Doctrinal and Philosophical Dimensions

What people believe about the origins of the world, the meaning of suffering and evil and who the *Buddha* or Jesus are, is usually rooted in the narratives of their own religions, and they will often test this in their own experience. This is another example of how it is not possible to talk about one dimension without referring to others and the balance and emphasis differs in different religions. Often Western, Christian-influenced studies of religions have exaggerated the importance of beliefs, whilst from an Indian perspective, practice or actions might be more important. The doctrinal dimension engages the intellectual, cognitive side of human beings and has therefore produced work in philosophy of religion, for example Christian philosophical theology or Buddhist studies on *Sunyata* (emptiness or spaciousness).

The Ethical and Legal Dimension

The moral dimension of religions is set down in precepts, rules and commandments and these are often rooted in sacred scriptures and the stories of the faiths. For many, ethics are the centre of religious life, loving the neighbour the touchstone of religious committment. For others, they are foundational for making any spiritual progress and includes concern for the whole natural world. Ethics are most commonly expressed in communities, which links this dimension with the next.

The Social and Institutional Dimension

Richard Gombrich pointed out that religion is as much about belonging as believing. People have a strong sense of the group of which they are a part, whether that is the Christian *Church* locally or world-wide, the Buddhist *Sangha*, the People of Israel or the *Umma* (Muslim Community). To understand a faith we need to see how it works amongst an actual group of people. This will be the dimension of religion that will be of most interest to sociologists and social anthropologists (see Part II Chapters 6 and 7), whilst the psychologist (see Part II Chapter 8) might be more interested in the experiential dimension and the philosopher in the belief dimension (see Part II Chapter 5).

The Material or Aesthetic Dimension

Most religions have some sense of natural or human-made sacred places and have sought to create beautiful visual art, architecture, dance and music to evoke and express something of their beliefs and experience. For example, Muslims are forbidden to create representational religious art, but use beautiful calligraphy to enhance the *Qur'an* as The Word of God and use abstract patterns which point the worshipper to the complex harmony of *Allah*'s creation. Hindus both paint and sculpt many aspects of the Divine, both male, female and imaginary creatures which are 'fingers pointing to Reality' and, in the words of Rudolf Otto, express or evoke in the worshipper a sense of awe in what is as marvellous as the 'the light of a thousand suns' (see *Bhagavad Gita* Chapter 11).

Ninian Smart suggests that this kind of model of religions gives a balanced picture of what religious life involves. It does not neglect either ideas or practices; the importance of individuals or communities; historical traditions or innovative experiences. It can also be applied to worldviews that are not religious. In a little book he wrote called *Mao* (now out of print) he has a final chapter on Mao as a religious leader, using his early six-dimensional model as a basis for discussion.

Another model of religion can be found in *Understanding Religion* by Eric Sharpe (1933–2000 CE). He interacts with Smart's ideas and suggests that religion has four functional modes. Sharpe, like our other authors, points out that religion is not a simple thing and does not fulfil one single function or need, but is multi-functional. In looking at religions in this way he says he is setting aside the philosophical and theological questions about the essence of religions and looking not at what functions religion ought to fulfil but what it actually does fulfil under varying circumstances. To do this he appreciates that a great deal has to be known factually about the religious life of humankind and that the work of the whole range of scholars who have traditionally studied religions (psychologists, sociologists, philologists, historians and so on – see

Part II) have a part to play in presenting a rounded picture. He does not claim complete originality for his scheme and refers to an early version of Smart's dimensions as an alternative pattern, recognising that dimension and function are different kinds of terms (1983: 95).

My fourfold scheme I should therefore like to present as follows: religion operates, humanly speaking, in four functional modes. Opinions may differ as to what to call them, but we may perhaps use the labels:

1. Existential

2. Intellectual

3. Institutional

4. Ethical

Sharpe explains how, in his view, in the life of an individual or community, one mode is often more central than others. Like Smart he considers that other human value systems such as Marxism or *humanism* can be analysed in the same way, and that the modes cannot exist in isolation from each other. He describes them in the following ways (1983: 97ff.).

The Existential Mode: The Circle of Faith

This is the purely individual aspect of religion: the dominant factor here is the unquestioning acceptance of the reality of the supernatural/transcendent order (under whatever set of images), and a sense of dependence upon and trust in the influence of that order. It involves the emotions and the will, faith, trust, love, fear, devotion, confidence, security.

The Intellectual Mode: The Circle of Beliefs

This mode involves the formulation of statements about the supernatural or transcendent order. These beliefs are assented to by individuals and groups within the faiths. This is the arena of doctrines, dogmas, theologies and philosophies, which are often originally based on experiences and revelations. People and communities articulate beliefs to communicate with later generations and outsiders and to say what the tradition does not contain if there are variations at any given time.

The Institutional Mode: The Circle of Organisations

Religions include both natural organisations such as families and nations, and social groups that are entirely based on choice, a community of believers. Sharpe points out that the voluntary principle is both recent and local, by which he means post-*Reformation* Christian and Western. In many religions, for example Judaism, Zoroastrianism (Parsi) and Hinduism, membership comes when you are born into your religious community.

The Ethical Mode: The Circle of Duties

In many religious traditions ethics are inseparable from an understanding of the totality of religious life. In the recent west, ethics have become more separated out from other aspects of religion and given a more central place as an essence or common core. As with the other modes, ethics need to be seen as intertwined with experience, beliefs and community. For example, what a person believes about the relationship of human beings to the rest of the animal and plant world will affect their attitudes to environmental issues.

3. MORE RECENT DEFINITIONS

Other scholars have continued to add to these ideas and in a university course you will enter into this debate about and search for an adequate understanding of the complex and diverse phenomenon that is religion. The anthropologist Clifford Geertz sees religion as a 'cultural system' (Geertz,

1973) and Timothy Fitzgerald also wants to emphasise that the object of our study is culture, understood as the system of values, and the interpretation of symbolic systems, including the ritualisation of everyday life and the legitimisation of power (Fitzgerald, 2000). In thirteen theses presented at a meeting of the American Academy of Religion in 1995, Bruce Lincoln says

> religion is that discourse whose defining characteristic is its desire to speak of things eternal and transcendent with an authority equally transcendent and eternal. History, in the sharpest possible contrast, is that discourse which speaks of things temporal and terrestial in a human and fallible voice, while staking its claim to authority on rigorous critical practice (quoted in McCutcheon (ed.), 1999: 395).

Seth Kunin suggests that our definitions are socially and culturally constructed and gives the following as a provisional understanding: 'Religion is any shared totalising system of relating to or understanding the world (in a literal or non-literal sense)' (Kunin, 2003: 221).

It is important to remember that the models and definitions suggested by scholars are ways of describing religions rather than methods for studying them, though they may be linked to certain approaches. In Section II, we shall turn to the issues involved in the methods used, of how we study religions, but before that, in the next chapter, we shall look at the various ways in which scholars group religions.

BIBLIOGRAPHY

Bowker, John (ed.) (1997), *The Oxford Dictionary of World Religions*, Oxford: Oxford University Press.

Cooper, David (1996), *World Philosophies: An Historical Introduction*, Oxford: Blackwell.

Fitzgerald, Timothy (2000), *The Ideology of Religious Studies*, New York and Oxford: Oxford University Press.

Geertz, Clifford (1973), *Interpretation of Cultures*, New York: Basic Books.

Gombrich, Richard (1997), *What Kind of Thing is Religion?* article in *World Religions in Education*, the annual journal of the Shap Working Party London SW1P 3XF.

Hardy, Alister [1979] (1997 paperback ed.), *The Spiritual Nature of Man*, The Religious Experience Research Centre, University of Wales, Lampeter SA48 7ED.

Keown, Damien (1996), *Buddhism: A Very Short Introduction*, Oxford: Oxford University Press.

Kunin, Seth (2003), *Religion: The Modern Theories*, Edinburgh: Edinburgh University Press.

McCutcheon, Russell T. (1999), *The Insider/Outsider Problem in The Study of Religion: A Reader*, London: Cassell.

Otto, Rudolf [1917, *Das Heilege*: 1923 tr.] (1950 tr. Harvey, J.), *The Idea of the Holy*, Oxford: Oxford University Press.

Sharpe, Eric (1983), *Understanding Religion*, London: Duckworth.

Smart, Ninian (1974), *Mao*, London: Fontana.

Smart, Ninian (1999), *World Philosophies*, London: Routledge.

Smith, Wilfred Cantwell (1978), *The Meaning and End of Religion*, London: SPCK.

Woodhead, Linda *et al.* (2002), *Religions in the Modern World*, London: Routledge.

2. GROUPING RELIGIONS

1. INTRODUCTION

Firstly, it is important to note that the way in which university courses, teachers and books group religions will depend on what they count as a religion and which religions are considered important (see Part I Chapter 1). We have included in this chapter examples of worldviews or lifeways and religions which are no longer institutionally active to keep the field broad and provoke discussion. We would like you to develop the confidence to challenge labels and groupings and ask questions. For example, do syllabuses use the term 'non-Christian religions', which suggests that Christianity is the norm for thinking about things (see Part II Chapter 3)? Also note where AD (from the Latin 'in the year of our Lord') and BC (before Christ) are used in datings, for although the numerical calculation of this system is now the international convention, the terminology used in religious studies is CE (common era) and BCE (before the common era), which are more neutrally descriptive terms. Most religions also have their own dating and years may not be the same length, as in the case of Islam (see section 4.5).

2. TYPOLOGIES

2.1 World religions

One common grouping is to talk about the 'world' (or even in the past 'great') religions, which usually means those which have lasted for a long time and in that time travelled and transplanted themselves across the globe in various ways. These transplantations may be through deliberate missionary activity or colonialism (as in the case of Christianity and Islam), or through persecution and exile (as in the case of Judaism or both Hindu and Sikh Ugandan Asians), through trade routes (as in the case of Buddhists travelling to China along the silk road) and economic migration. Transplantation and migration have brought what are now commonly called *diasporas*, which are a focus of many contemporary studies (Hinnells (ed.), 2005: Chapter 30). The so-called 'world' religions can also be called 'scriptural' religions, since they all now have written texts that can be studied. A chart which picks up this term and the alternative group might look like this. Some of the terms are also important in anthropological studies (see Part II Chapter 6).

World	Local
great	little/tribal
scriptural	oral or pre-literate
global	indigenous or local
classical	popular

All of these terms can be and should be challenged. For example, most of the sacred teachings of the 'great' traditions were orally transmitted before they were written down, in some cases for centuries. Hinduism has its roots in the *indigenous* traditions of India (see sections 2.3 and 4.1), Whilst Judaism can be seen as a tribal tradition at its origins (see section 4.2). Christianity was once a New Religious Movement within Judaism (see section 4.4) and Buddhism (see section 4.3) and the *Jains* emerged as new movements from Brahminism, which is an early form of a strand of Hinduism. The situation is always changing and new movements are still developing and may become 'great' traditions in the future. For example, an academic conference was held a few years ago with the title *Mormonism, The Next World Religion?* Also many little, oral and popular local traditions are practised within and blended with the 'great, world, classical, scriptural' traditions such as Buddhism (the spirit cults of north-east Thailand) and

Christianity (the *indigenous pagan* practices of Europe such as decorating evergreen trees at Christmas, using mistletoe and the name of Easter which comes from the pagan goddess Eostre). *Indigenous* traditions are also now transnational and have their diasporas world-wide, for example the communities of *Maoris* in London.

2.2 Religions of historical interest

This group of religions can also be called the classical, ancient or even 'dead' traditions. Of course, all religions are of historical interest and the field was for many years called The History of Religions; the International Association for scholars in the subject still uses that name. However, in this section we are referring to religions which have been very influential but have ceased to exist as strong separate entities. That there is such a group is implied when people use the opposite phrase 'living religions' (Hinnells (ed.), 2000). However, very few religions that were once practised have completely disappeared. For example, the religions that were the focus of Romans and Greeks and Norsemen have survived in the shape of many Christian churches, sacred sites and the names of months, days and festivals in Europe, and the techniques and style of Egyptian burial portraits were adopted by Christian icon painters. Old practices tend to be absorbed and blended into the newer traditions which, for reasons of power, or popular transplantation, become dominant. There can also be a recovering of ancient traditions as we have seen in Europe in the emergence of neo *paganisms*, including *animism*.

2.3 Indigenous traditions

There was a time when early anthropologists used terms such as *primitive* to describe local traditions. Even though some, for example Evans Pritchard, said they used *primitive* in a value-free sense, it has a pejorative ring, indicating something inferior, and indeed some European researchers thought that this was the case (see Part II Chapter 6). Alternative terms, such as primal or primary, which seem to suggest that these are the earliest forms of human religious life, and tribal, also now seem unsatisfactory. So *indigenous* has become the more scholarly name for those local beliefs and practices of, for example, small traditional communities in Africa and the first nation peoples of North America (also called North American Indians) and the Pacific islanders. But there is not a hard separating line between the categories that we use, and *indigenous* practices have now influenced and become part of 'world' religions in most places. For example, many North American Christians integrate positively into their *spirituality* insights from the first nation peoples (the preferred insider term) and traditional practices are often a part of African Christianity. We can also see Shinto, the way of the sacred powers or kami, as the *indigenous* tradition of Japan and Hinduism as originally the *indigenous* religion of India. *Paganism(s)* make up the old, *indigenous* religions of Europe and we can add to the list Australian aboriginal, *Maori* and other first-nation traditions such as those of the North and Southern American Indians.

2.4 New Religious Movements

This is a relatively new term introduced by sociologists and suggests movements which emerge, often from a 'world' religion, but which have a somewhat separate and often a controversial status from the viewpoint of the host religion. Another term that is sometimes used is 'alternative religious tradition'. Both of these phrases attempt to be descriptive and scholars of religions try to avoid the terms *sect* and *cult* because they have a pejorative/critical/normative ring, that is they state from the point of view of the host religion or society at large that these are heretical, breakaway and marginalised minority groups. Although the phrase New Religious Movement (NRM) is quite new, there are examples from early times to which the term can be applied. For example, as we have already suggested, Christianity can be seen at its origins as an NRM emerging out of rabbinic Judaism, and Jainism emerged like Buddhism from a Brahminical Hindu environment. The *Bahai* faith has been seen as an heretical *sect* of Islam in its origins and Guru Nanak, the first Sikh *guru*, was critical of both Hindu and Muslim attitudes in his day. All of these have become 'world' religions. NRMs, however, do not always separate from the host religion. Some NRMs, like the *Methodists* and *Quakers,* have remained within Christianity and are now known by the more mainstream and 'insider' term of 'denomination', whilst the *Unitarians* and the *Unification Church* (*Moonies*) are still viewed by many mainstream Christians as 'outside'. Most now see the 'party of Ali', or *Shi'a* Islam, as one of the two main strands of this world religion. Against a Hindu background, *ISKCON,* The International Society for Krishna Consciousness (*Hare Krishnas*), is interesting because, although it is studied as an NRM, the practice and ideas which make it distinctive go back to the Indian teacher Chaitanya (1486–1533 CE). The 'insider' Hindu term *sampradaya* can be used of both *ISKCON* and the *Swaminarayan* movement, whilst there are other movements such as the *Valmikis* which are more controversial both to Hindus and Sikhs whose traditions they bridge and blend. Other Indian/Hindu derived movements such as the *Brahma Kumaris* prefer to be seen as a spiritual university rather than a Hindu religious movement. In Japan there are not only many new movements, though some like *Soka Gakkai* have their roots in the teachings of the Japanese Buddhist teacher Nichiren (1222–82 CE), but also what are called new, new religious movements.

3.   GEOGRAPHICAL GROUPINGS

Geographical descriptions such as 'east' and 'west' depend on where you are standing and, as with many other terms, assume a European perspective, which is where the field of the study of religions first developed (see Part II Chapter 3). We can criticise this grouping not only because of the European and North American stance in the terms 'east' and 'west', but also because many of these religions, wherever they began, are now transcultural and global and have significant *diasporas*. So 'east' and 'west' apply only to where they began. Another way we can group traditions is with more specific reference to continents or sub-continents and we can then distinguish between where they began and where they are now. An example might be placing Buddhism as an Indian religion, which is where it began, but since there were many centuries when it died out in India but was a significant presence in China and Japan and is now world-wide, the label 'Indian' is rather limited. Most of the traditions are now present in *diasporas*, that is they are transplanted to most parts of the world. So studying religions in the UK, for example, necessitates looking at neo-*paganism* in Wales; *Maoris* in London; Hindus in Leeds; *Jains* in Leicester; Buddhists in Dumfries; Sikhs in Southall and so on. Try making your own list of religions present in other geographical areas, such as contemporary Japan, North and South America or the Caribbean.

4. SPECIFIC WORLD RELIGIONS

In what follows we shall look at issues in the study of the so-called world religions rather than just give a survey of each. No attempt has been made to give statistics of the numbers in any tradition, since there are considerable problems in obtaining such statistics and they are always changing. If you are interested in the numbers in the UK, the most recent census figures are interesting, but do not cover the complete range of traditions (see Part II Chapter 9 section 3).

4.1 Hinduisms

The name 'Hinduism' is used for a way of life which is rooted in the traditional, or *indigenous*, religions of India. These roots, though not the term 'Hinduism', go so far back into Indian traditional ideas and practices that no date can be given for their beginning and it is only the archeological evidence in the valley of the River Indus that gives clues about early practices such as ritual bathing, *yoga* and a focus on the *goddess*. There is no single founder and elements became blended with the beliefs and practices of the group usually called the *Aryans*. They were outsiders and brought into India with them, as far back as the second millennium BCE, oral traditions which were the early versions of what became the most sacred texts of Hinduism, the *Vedas* in Vedic Sanskrit. However, these are not the most studied or used texts from the point of view of the majority of practising Hindus, but are the domain of the *brahmins* (priests). There also developed a class (*varna*) structure in which the *brahmins* were the spiritually superior and whose rituals validated the status of the rulers, the kshatriyas (warriors/rulers), the materially supreme and patrons of the brahminical rituals, the vaishyas (artisans) and shudras (peasants). They counted other groups as outside the system (outcastes, called harijans by Gandhi (1869–1948 CE), and scheduled classes in post-independence India where discrimination is illegal). There are also many people in India who follow tribal religions which are quite separate from Hinduisms. The ancientness of the traditional religions of India, which have within them a great variety of practices and ideas with no central authority, developed and accumulated over four thousand years of history. This has led writers such as Sarvapelli Radhakrishnan (1888–1975 CE) to use the phrase *sanatana dharma*, eternal truth, as an alternative name to 'Hinduism'. It was the Persians who first used the term 'Hindu', or 'Sindhu', for those who belonged to the religion of the land round the Indus and in the nineteenth century reforming figures such as Ram Mohan Roy (1772–1833 CE), responding to the criticisms of the British missionary and colonial presence, presented 'Hinduism' as a more Western-style single religion.

So closely have Hinduisms been associated with Indian identity (over 80 per cent of people in the modern state of India count themselves as Hindus) that if one asks 'Who is a Hindu?' the answer may be that a Hindu is a person born into a Hindu family, or someone who has a particular way of life as an Indian, more than someone who holds a particular set of beliefs. There is considerable flexibility and diversity for those who count themselves as Hindus and in the twentieth century, mainly through the Hindu NRMs such as *ISKCON* and the *Ramakrishna Vedanta Mission*, people converted to Hinduism. The emphasis in Hindu living may be on deeds (*karma*), both ethical and ritual, which affect one's rebirth in *samsara*. It is also possible to choose which *istadevata* (personal God) on which to focus one's devotion (*bhakti*) and to worship God in the form of the Mahadevi (Great Mother *Goddess* in the form of the gentle Lakshmi or Parvati or fierce Durga or Kali). Other popular forms are the *avatars* of Vishnu. One *avatar* is called Krishna, whose story is told in the *Bhagavad Gita*, which is the most popular, though not the most sacred, text of Hinduism and part of the great epic, the *Mahabharata*, and in the *Bhagavata Puranas*. Another *avatar* is Rama, whose story, with that of his wife Sita, an *avatar* of Lakshmi, is in the *Ramayana*. Shiva is also important for many Hindus as the focus of devotion.

In Hinduism there are six *darshanas* (viewpoints) which count as *orthodox* and the views within these are diverse and even contradictory. One viewpoint is *Advaita Vedanta*, whose great founding thinker was Shankara (c. 788–850 CE). This is the philosophical school to which Sarvapelli Radhakrishnan belonged. He, and through him *Advaita Vedanta* ideas, have influenced what many Westerners think Hinduism is. In this approach spiritual, experiential knowledge (*jnana*) is central to the movement towards *moksha* (liberation) which is envisaged not as an eternal loving relationship with the Beloved as in the *bhakti* movements, but as becoming one with that of which you are already a part, *Brahman*. This is the famous identification of the *atman* (the self or soul within all beings) with *Brahman* (the ultimate transpersonal Reality) stated so classically in the texts called the *Upanishads*. The variety of Hindu *sampradayas* and the growth of NRMs along with changes amongst those in the Hindu *diasporas* make the study of the above and other Hinduisms a constantly developing area.

4.2 Judaisms

As has already been suggested, Judaism can be seen as a tribal religion at its origins. However, its own dating of 5767 in 2006 CE, which is celebrated at the new year festival of *Rosh Hashanah*, looks back to the creation of the world (remembered also in the joy of Shabbat – Sabbath – the weekly day of rest) and of the first human beings, before there was a tribe of Judah and any 'Jewish' people. So Jewish people suggest that the focus of their faith is the welfare of all creation in which the Jewish people have been given a special responsibility. Although in the Liberal or *Reform* traditions of modern Judaism (another term used in the USA is Progressive), it is possible to convert to Judaism, or to be Jewish through having a Jewish father, the *Orthodox* definition of who is Jewish is someone born of a Jewish mother. Ceremonies such as circumcision at eight days old for boys, bar mitzvah at thirteen for boys and bat mitzvah at twelve for girls only confirm existing Jewish identity. The emphasis for all Jews is on 'religion' as a way of life and ethics rather than beliefs. Many Jewish celebrations take place in the home rather than the place of community gathering, called the *synagogue*. The norm in Judaism is married life and the appreciation and proper care for the material world that is God-given.

The central texts of Judaism are the *Torah* (Teaching/Law), the *Neviim* (Prophets) and the *Ketuvim* (Writings), also collectively called *Tenakh*. These terms are transliterations from the Hebrew language, which has its own alphabet, and (as with all transliterated terms) words are sometimes spelt differently in different English books. The *Tenakh* covers what Christians call 'The Old Testament', which is an inappropriate term for Jewish insiders, as is the incorrect term 'Jahweh' for God. Jews refer to God by the term Ha Shem (the name).

The above texts are listed in order of sacredness, but it is not possible to understand any Jewish life without the *Talmud* (the classical collection is the Babylonian *Talmud* of about 600 CE), which contains the Mishnah and the whole range of, Rabbinic teachings and interpretations of the *Torah* through the ages, a tradition of interpretation which is still taking place. It is the growth of rabbinic Judaism, developed in the context of exile and *diasporas*, that has determined contemporary Jewish life.

Key figures in Jewish history are Abraham, seen by Jews, Muslims and Christians as the first monotheist and a great example of a person of faith; Moses, who led the people out of Egypt and received the law on Sinai; the priest and scribe Ezra who re-established the Jerusalem Temple and community after the exile in Babylon in the sixth century BCE, and David, the ideal of a ruler who acknowledged God's law. Key women are Sarah, the mother of the nation; Deborah, the prophetess who led the people into battle; Ruth the Moabitess, who was such a loyal daughter-in-law and an ancestress of David and Esther, who helped to save her people and whose story is in the scroll of Esther read at the festival of *Purim*. The prophets such as Amos, Hosea and Isaiah are also important as people who reminded kings, priests and Israelites of the faith they should be living.

Three central festivals of Judaism are *Pesach* (Passover), *Sukkot* (Tabernacles) and Simchat Torah, which all look back to the story of freedom from slavery in the Exodus from Egypt, the wilderness wandering and the gift of the *Torah*. At these and at *Yom Kippur* (the Day of Atonement) the themes are both specific, related to the history of a people, and universal – those of oppression and freedom, repentence and forgiveness.

The term *diaspora*, which is now used of the movements of many religions away from their traditional homelands, originates in the study of Jewish history. Jews were exiled to Babylon in 586–538 BCE and Jewish communities also moved for trade and other reasons across the Mediterranean in the time of the Roman Empire. In 70 CE the Romans exiled the

Jews from their homeland and there followed an extensive tradition of 'wandering'. During the *diaspora*, periods of prosperity in various countries such as Spain and Germany have been followed by persecution (for example the *Shoah* under the Nazis), expulsion and migration. This made the establishment of a right to return to the state of Israel after 1948 very important.

There are, as with the other traditions, various kinds of Judaism. The first division, which is an old one, is between the Ashkenazim and Sephardim. The Ashkenazim are the descendants of the Jews who settled in Central and Eastern Europe and their main language was Yiddish, which is a mixture of German and Hebrew. The *Shoah* (commonly called the Holocaust) in Nazi Germany destroyed much of their culture, but those who were able to leave sustained their way of life in Israel, North America and the UK. The Sephardim are the descendants of the Jewish communities of Spain and Portugal and their main language, Ladino, was a mixture of Spanish and Hebrew. They were expelled from Spain in 1492 and lived in Turkey, North Africa and Italy, migrating into Northern Europe from the sixteenth century, and then to America and other parts. Each group has its own style of music, customs, synagogue decoration and interpretations and Sephardic art is much influenced by Islamic cultures.

Other divisions are called by slightly different names in the UK and the USA. There are the Ultra-*Orthodox* Hasidim (Hebrew for 'faithful ones'), whose dress is that of eighteenth-century Poland where the groups began under charismatic teachers, or rebbes. There are the *Orthodox* who retain Hebrew for their synagogue services and believe that *Torah* should be followed exactly as the word of God. In the UK the term *Reform* covers a spectrum of those more or less liberal in their interpretation of the 'spirit' rather than the letter of the law. They have women rabbis and the majority of their worship is in English. The roots of the *Reform* movements are in the eighteenth-century European *Enlightenment*. In the USA terms such as 'progressive' and 'conservative' are used and there are also newer groups such as reconstructionists.

4.3   Buddhisms

The key figure at the historical beginnings of Buddhism (Siddhartha Gautama) lived in north-east India in the fifth century BCE. The pattern of his life, from leaving the security of his home in response to the four sights, old age, sickness, death and a holy man, to his enlightenment, has become a model for Buddhists. The title *Buddha* means an enlightened being. The Buddhist community (*sangha*) is made up of male and female renouncers who live on the gifts of alms given by female and male householders who see the monks and nuns as living close to the *Buddha*'s ideals of selflessness and renuncia- tion. The *Buddha*'s teachings are in the *Pali Canon*, or Tripitaka. These were originally three baskets (pitakas) of texts written on palm leaves, which contain sayings (sutta/sutra); the code of monastic discipline (vinaya) and further explanations (abhidhamma/abhidharma). Much reflects the *Buddha*'s engagement with the teachings and practices of the *Brahmin* priests of his time. For example, the *Buddha* suggests that, instead of lighting three ritual fires each day, the *Brahmins* should be blowing out fires; however, he says that the fires to which he is referring are the fires of greed, hatred and ignorance. This illustrates what is seen as the move away from ritual towards inwardness which is characteristic of the Buddhist path, including an emphasis on intention in the making of ethical decisions. It also provides the imagery of 'blown out' or 'cooling' for the indescribable state of Nibbana/*Nirvana*, which is the only permanent state, the tran- scendent reality for Buddhists. Life in *samsara* (the cycle of rebirth, a term also used by Hindus and Sikhs) is characterised in particular by impermanence and can be transcended through developing generosity and compassion, morality, meditation and wisdom. The last three are developed into the famous noble eightfold path, which is the fourth of the Four Noble

Truths. These describe life as suffering or unsatisfactory and see this as rooted in thirst, an image for desire and craving. They teach that it is possible for these to cease if people follow the path. The Four Noble Truths are:

1. The truth of suffering

2. The truth of the arising of suffering in craving

3. The truth of the cessation of suffering

4. The path out of suffering, which is an eightfold path in three parts, wisdom, morality and meditation:

1 and 2 Right or appropriate understanding and resolve (wisdom)

3, 4 and 5 Right or appropriate speech, action and livelihood (morality)

6, 7 and 8 Right or appropriate effort, mindfulness and meditation (meditation)

The Buddha encouraged his followers to teach in the local dialects of the people instead of the Sanskrit which was the sacred language of Brahminism. He himself was not a *Brahmin* but traditionally seen as on a par with the kshatriya, or princely class. Since his time Buddhists have translated their teachings into the languages of the many countries where Buddhists have travelled, classically to Sri Lanka (Ceylon), Thailand (Siam) and Myanmar (Burma), which are the countries that belong to the conservative *Theravada* forms of Southern Buddhism. In Tibet, China, Korea and Japan, the *Mahayana*, the Northern and Far Eastern practices of the Tibetan, Zen and Pure Land Schools have grown. Texts have extended beyond the *Pali Canon* and its translation to many others such as the Prajnaparamita (Perfection of Wisdom Sutras) and Saddharmapundarika (Lotus Sutra). All forms of Buddhism and many new movements such as The Friends of The Western Buddhist Order, Soka Gakkai, Rissho Kosei Kai,

in the twentieth century either developed in or travelled to
Europe, the USA and South America, South Africa and other
parts of the world. This was the result of colonial and scholarly interest, economic migration of peoples and the migration of many Tibetans after 1959. Many Westerners became
Buddhists through 'taking refuge' in the *Buddha*, *Dharma*
(Teaching) and *Sangha* (community), and in addition for
Tibetans, the *Lama* (spiritual teacher). There is also the suggestion that we should now add 'Western' to the categories of
northern and southern Buddhism and even talk of a Navayana,
a new path. In the twentieth century controversial forms of
Buddhism which are 'socially engaged' and which some scholars have called 'Protestant Buddhism' challenged the stereotype
of Buddhism as 'world-denying and other-worldly'.

4.4   Christianities

The focus of Christianity, both historically and doctrinally, is
Jesus *Christ* (current dates for his life are 4 BCE–29 CE),
who was born and died within Judaism. His title *Christ* is an
anglicised form of the Greek 'Christos', which translates
the Hebrew term 'Messiah', the Anointed One, a title for the
hoped-for leader who will change the world to a place of peace
and justice and whose coming the Jewish people still hope for.

Jesus' teaching that the Kingdom of God was stirring
among and within the people who followed him and his chal-
lenging of many of the Jewish teachers and leaders of his time
brought hostility from both the Jewish establishment and the
Roman occupying power who were always alert to protest
movements. Many ordinary Jewish people, though, were his
close followers. The Romans ordered his crucifixion and tradition says that they put the label 'King of the Jews' over the
cross. Jesus can be seen historically as a Jewish *rabbi* and
prophetic reformer and the movement of his followers as a
Jewish New Religious Movement which later, under the theological influence of figures such as Paul and the early *church*
councils such as Nicaea (325 CE) and Chalcedon (451 CE) and

the political influence of the Emperor Constantine (288–357 CE), became a separate and state religion. Christians' understanding of the figure of Jesus also extended to seeing him as the incarnation of God, fully God as well as fully human, and his death upon the cross as a sacrifice which repairs the broken relationship between God and human beings, an idea called the *Atonement*. Christian statements of faith or creeds see God in three relational aspects: Father, Son and Holy Spirit, together called the Trinity.

Christianity became a missionary religion very soon after its beginnings and began to include, through *baptism*, members from outside Judaism. Its scriptures were accounts of Jesus' life (*Gospels*) and letters of various followers of Jesus, including the influential Paul. These became known as the *New Testament*, with the Jewish *Tenakh* included under the Christian title 'Old Testament' to make the *Bible*. Christianity spread to Rome, the centre of the Roman Empire, where it is said one of Jesus' closest early followers, Peter, was crucified. He became the founding father of the Roman church (the first bishop of Rome and *Pope*). The *Pope* is still the most senior figure of authority for *Roman Catholic* Christians. Those whose tradition developed in the other great imperial centre, Byzantium or Constantinople (named after Constantine, now Istanbul), believe that the bishops of all the ancient centres have equal authority and they developed into the *Eastern Orthodox* Churches of Byzantium, Russia, Greece and other geographical areas.

In the sixteenth century in Europe under the influence of figures such as Luther (1483–1546 CE), Calvin (1509–64 CE) and Zwingli (1484–1531 CE) there were movements which saw the need for reform in the Western church. These reforms were based on the desire to have the *Bible* and the liturgies of the churches in the vernacular languages of the people instead of Latin and to have a religion based solely on faith and scripture rather than on the authority of Rome, works such as pilgrimage and buying indulgencies. These movements, which together brought about the *Reformation*, resulted in a third stream of Christianities, the *Protestant* churches which are varied and include Lutherans, Calvinists, *Anglicans*, *Baptists*, *Methodists* and many more, including those who see themselves as more radically reformed, such as the *Quakers*. There are also many Christian-linked NRMs, such as the *Jehovah's Witnesses*, *Mormons* and the *Unification Church* (*Moonies*). All forms of Christianity have spread over the whole world and some of the liveliest forms today are in the Pentecostal movements and in liberation theologies.

4.5 Islams

The Arabic name 'Islam' has within it the sense of peace, harmony and submission. The ideal for Muslims, those whose will is in harmony with the will of *Allah* (God), is that knowledge of *Allah*'s will which is embodied in the *Qur'an* (recitation) and example of the prophet Muhammad (recorded in the *Hadith*) will lead them to live in harmony and responsibility with fellow human beings and all of *Allah*'s creation. Humans are *khalifah* (viceregents), a term which is paralleled by the Hebrew scriptures' idea that humans have stewardship under God of the created world.

Muhammad (c. 570–632 CE) was an orphan who at about the age of 40, after becoming a successful and respected trader, had an experience of receiving the Word of God in Arabic through the angel Jibril (Gabriel), at first on Mount Hira and then in other experiences through the rest of his life. These carefully memorised teachings became the written *Qur'an*, which Muslims believe has remained unchanged throughout Islamic history. Muhammad is seen as the final prophet (the seal of the prophets) in a long line of prophets, who include Adam, Abraham, Moses and Jesus. All of the prophets knew *Allah*'s teachings that there is only One God. After all their names Muslims say 'peace be upon him'. The receiving of the *Qur'an*, Muslims believe, is a correction of the misunderstood and misremembered, but originally the same, word given to Moses in the *Torah* and taught by Jesus in the Injil (*Gospel*).

After he received his call to be a prophet, Muhammad taught in Makka (Mecca) that there is only One God. In Makka the religion was a pagan polytheism and idolatry and he experienced much hostility from the people. He was invited to move to Madina and Islam dates itself from this migration and the founding of the first Muslim community (*Umma*) in 622 CE. He later returned to Makka to rule in the name of *Allah* and died in 632 CE. After his death, four so-called 'rightly guided' *khalifas* (caliphs) ruled the community and Islam spread, but there were arguments over who should be the true ruler and those of the Shi'at Ali (the party of Ali, Muhammad's cousin and son-in-law, called *Shi'a* Islam) thought that he and his sons Hasan and Hussein, who were the prophet's grandsons, were the rightful leaders of the community, especially when Hussein pitted himself with a small army against the might of the Ummayad *khalifa* and the majority (*sunni* traditionalists) and was massacred at Kerbala (680 CE), an event which became a symbol for *Shi'as* of the innocent suffering of the righteous. There are also *sufi* (mystic) groups in both *Sunni* (the traditionalists who are the majority) and *Shi'a* movements. *Sufis* experience such closeness to *Allah* and such a sense of God in all created things that other Muslims have sometimes accused them of shirk (associating with God what is not God).

Key female role models for Muslims are Khadija, the mature, established businesswoman who was Muhammad's first wife; A'isha, the lively young woman whom he married after Khadija died and who rode with the troops in battle and spoke in the assembly, and the woman mystic Rabi'a, who spoke of loving God for himself alone, neither out of fear of hell nor hope of heaven.

Muslims follow the example of Muhammad recorded in the collections of his sayings and deeds (the *Hadith* and *Sunnah*), which, with the *Qur'an,* make up the *Shari'a(h).* Their lives are based on the five pillars. These are:

- the profession of faith (iman) that there is no God but *Allah* and Muhammad is his prophet (the **shahada**)
- prayer (**salat**) five times a day

- fasting (**sawn** or **sawm**) in the month of Ramadan
- almsgiving (**zakat**)
- pilgrimage (*hajj*) to Makka at least once in a lifetime

As Islam has spread across the world it has often adapted to local custom, and women's dress, along with the styles of *mosques* (places of prostration), are diverse in this way of life in which God is concerned about what you eat, what you wear and who you marry.

4.6   Sikhisms

The founding historical *guru* (spiritual teacher) for Sikhs (learners or disciples) is Guru Nanak (1469–1539 CE), who lived in the Punjab in India and interacted with those of both Hindu and Muslim traditions around him, questioning that these labels exist for God. His teachings, those of earlier and later Indian saint/mystics and those of the later Sikh *gurus* are collected by the tenth and last historical *guru*, Gobind Singh, into the *Guru Granth Sahib* (also called the *Adi Granth*). After his death the *Guru Granth Sahib* becomes the teacher of the community and where it is enthroned becomes a *gurdwara*, a Sikh place of worship, the gateway to the *guru*, who is One God and Wonderful Lord and with whom the Sikh has a relationship of loving devotion.

The Ten Human *Gurus*	
Guru Nanak	1469–1539 CE
Guru Angad	1504–1542 CE (*guru* from 1539)
Guru Amar Das	1479–1574 CE (*guru* from 1552)
Guru Ram Das	1534–1581 CE (*guru* from 1574)
Guru Arjan	1563–1606 CE (*guru* from 1581)
Guru Hargobind	1595–1644 CE (*guru* from 1606)
Guru Rai	1630–1661 CE (*guru* from 1644)
Guru Har Krishnan	1656–1664 CE (*guru* from 1661)
Guru Tegh Bahadur	1621–1675 CE (*guru* from 1664)
Guru Gobind Singh	1666–1708 CE (*guru* from 1675)

Devotional songs (*kirtan*) and remembrance of the divine names (nam simaran) are a feature of Sikh worship. Wherever the *Guru Granth Sahib* is enthroned there is open hospitality for all who want to come to the *langar*, the *guru*'s kitchen. Its availability cuts across all social, racial and religious divides. All the important events of a Sikh's life, such as naming a child and marriage, are centred on the *Guru Granth Sahib*. People count themselves Sikh by birth and culture, but also make a very specific commitment in the ceremony of 'taking *amrit*' (a sweet substance) rooted in the act of *Guru* Gobind Singh in 1699 CE that founded the distinctive Sikh community (*khalsa*). A *khalsa* Sikh (fully initiated man or woman) wears 5 'Ks'. These are:

- **kes**, uncut hair, kept clean with a scarf or turban covering. This, and other bodily hair, is left as God intended it to grow

- **kangha**, a small comb to keep the hair neat, which shows spiritual discipline

- **kirpan**, a steel sword to defend what is right. This is often worn in a small and symbolic form

- **kara**, a steel bangle worn on the right wrist, a reminder of unity with God and the community

- **kachh**, long shorts, often now worn as an undergarment, but originally enabling the wearer to get up and act quickly when necessary

The model of life for Sikhs is marriage and family and any Sikh, man or woman, who is able and spiritually respected can become a *granthi*, one who reads the *Guru Granth Sahib* in the *Gurdwara*. Sikh men bear the name Singh (lion) and women Kaur (usually translated as 'princess').

The central Sikh sacred site is the city of Amritsar in the Punjab, where the fourth human *guru*, Ram Das, began the building of the *Harimandir* (called the Golden Temple) with its sacred pool in 1577 CE. This is where Sikhs often travel on pilgrimage.

BIBLIOGRAPHY

General

Bowker, John (ed.) (1997), *The Oxford Dictionary of World Religions*, Oxford: Oxford University Press.

Cohen, Robin (1997), *Global Diasporas: An Introduction*, London: Routledge.

Harvey, Graham (ed.) (2000), *Indigenous Religion: A Companion*, London: Cassell.

Hinnells, John R. (ed.) [1998] (2nd ed. 2000), *The New Penguin Handbook of Living Religions*, London: Penguin Books.

Morgan, Peggy and Clive Lawton (eds) [1996] (2nd ed. 2006), *Ethical Issues in Six Religious Traditions*, Edinburgh: Edinburgh University Press.

Shap Calendar of Religions from PO Box 38580, London SW1P 3XF.

Smart, Ninian and Richard Hecht (eds) [1982] (paperback ed. 1984), *Sacred Texts of The World*, London: Macmillan.

Woodhead, Linda *et al.* (2002), *Religions in the Modern World*, London: Routledge.

Hinduisms

Flood, Gavin (1996), *An Introduction to Hinduism*, Cambridge: Cambridge University Press.

Knott, Kim (1998), *Hinduism, A Very Short Introduction*, Oxford: Oxford University Press.

Suthren-Hirst, Jacqueline (1997), *Sita's Story*, Norwich: Religious and Moral Education Press.

Zaehner, R. C. (tr.) (1969), *The Bhagavad Gita*, Oxford: Oxford University Press.

Judaisms

Alexander, Philip S. (ed.) (1984), *Textual Sources for the Study of Judaism*, Manchester: Manchester University Press.

de Lange, Nicholas (2001), *An Introduction to Judaism*, Cambridge: Cambridge University Press.

Solomon, Norman (1996), *Judaism: A Very Short Introduction*, Oxford: Oxford University Press.

Wright, Melanie (2003), *Understanding Judaism*, Cambridge: Orchard Academic.

Buddhisms

Bechert, Heinz and Richard Gombrich (eds) [1984] (paperback ed. 1991), *The World of Buddhism*, London: Thames and Hudson.

Harvey, Peter (1990), *An Introduction to Buddhism*, Cambridge: Cambridge University Press.

Keown, Damien (1996), *Buddhism: A Very Short Introduction*, Oxford: Oxford University Press.

Lopez, Donald (ed.) (2004), *Buddhist Scriptures*, London: Penguin Books.

Christianities

The Bible: New International Version (1973), New Jersey: International Bible Society.

Davies, Douglas and Clare Drury (1997), *Themes and Issues in Christianity*, London: Cassell.

Weaver, Mary-Jo [1984] (2nd ed. 1991), *Introduction to Christianity*, Belmont, CA: Wadsworth.

Woodhead, Linda (2004), *Introduction to Christianity*, Cambridge: Cambridge University Press.

Islams

Esposito, John [1988] (revised 3rd ed. 2005), *Islam: The Straight Path*, Oxford: Oxford University Press.

Hamid, Abdul Wahid (1989), *Islam: The Natural Way*, London: MELS.

Pickthall, Muhammad M. (tr.) (1992), *The Meaning of the Glorious Koran*, New York: A. A. Knopf.

Rippin, Andrew [1990] (revised ed. 2000), *Muslims, Their Religious Beliefs and Practices*, London: Routledge.

Sikhs

Barrow, Joy (ed.) (1997), *Meeting Sikhs*, Leicester: Christians Aware.

Cole, W. Owen and Piara Singh Sambhi [1978] (1995 ed.), *The Sikhs: Their Religious Beliefs and Practices*, Brighton, Sussex Academic Press.

McLeod, W. H. (1989), *The Sikhs: History, Religion and Society*, New York: Columbia University Press.

Nesbitt, Eleanor and Gopinder Kaur (1999), *Guru Nanak*, Norwich: Religious and Moral Education Press.

PART II
Perspectives in the Study of Religions

PART II INTRODUCTION

One of the emphases in studying most subjects today is the diversity of perspectives or ways of approach that exist within each area. Some of these approaches are part of the history of subjects within particular cultural contexts. For example, text books a hundred years ago presented the voyages of Christopher Columbus to South America in a very positive light and now history books show the negative effects of his activities in relation to the peoples he 'discovered' and 'civilised'. We might also ask how the *indigenous* and first-nation peoples of Australia and North America view the European 'invaders'. Their voices on this matter are now being articulated and heard. People in each culture and historical period have their own perspectives on the 'other' and the issue of self and other, *insider* and *outsider* perspectives, is a key one in current studies. Alongside highlighting these issues belongs the debate about how we can, if we wish to, transcend our *insider* perspectives and understand the *insider* perspectives of the others. You will find that this is an interesting issue for phenomenologists, sociologists and anthropologists alike, who suggest and practise different ways of research which enables the 'crossing over'.

As well as diversity across history and cultures, there are also diverse perspectives amongst individual scholars, even those who have the same cultural background. They may debate fiercely with each other on issues such as why so many new or alternative religious movements were established in the late twentieth century. You will find these kinds of debates and issues in the books that you read, in the emphases of lecturers at universities and in the reflections of people with whom you talk.

The study of religions as a distinctive academic field which crosses disciplines is a relatively new subject area, though religions have been thought about and studied in different ways for centuries. Many prefer the phrase 'study of religions' to 'religious studies'; as the academic study of religions is not itself religious, it does not assume a religious perspective. The approaches and subject areas that contribute to the study of religions or religious studies are still developing and this adds vitality to the field. Philosophical approaches to religions have been established for many centuries, but psychologies, sociologies and anthropologies bring in relatively new methods, perspectives and questions. Equally a focus on *sciences* and religions (notice the plurals) is an emerging area of study, but one on which we do not have the space to focus, though other contemporarily important themes such as identity, which includes gender, are considered. We have also not included a section on the study of religions and the study of history, although historical perspectives and the history of religions make a very important contribution to understanding the changes that take place in religious traditions over time and how cultures have come into contact with each other and how this also effects change.

The key approaches in the field that are explored in Part II are presented with the knowledge that emphases and foci have changed and will change again over time. They are also not exhaustive as whole books and libraries have been written about each approach and others that we have not had the space to cover. No fixed and definitive positions are arrived at in the variety of approaches that are discussed; they are open-ended explorations and you will form your own judgements and in your undergraduate essays and seminars learn to argue a case for a viewpoint you have adopted, whether or not it is your own.

As well as courses on individual religions in departments of Religious Studies and Theology, you will also find that there are courses which include some focus on religion and religions in departments of oriental studies, sociology, anthropology, cultural studies, classics, history, law, art history and so on and that these departments may share some of their courses with religious studies, particularly if the university has a modular degree system. There are also courses specifically on anthropology of religions, sociology of religions and psychology of religions in departments of Religious Studies. Courses on how religion is studied with titles such as *The Nature of Religion* or *An Introduction to the Study of Religions* may focus on key thinkers who have attempted to define religion and laid foundations for its study. These are usually important figures in the history of the various approaches explored below, such as the anthropologist E. B. Tylor (1832–1917 CE); the sociologist Emile Durkheim (1858–1917 CE); the phenomenologist Mircea Eliade (1907–86 CE) and the psychologist Sigmund Freud (1856–1938 CE). Early thinkers often have their own theories about how religion began, for example in magic; in the worship of nature; in the belief in spirits (*animism*); in a tribal *totem* or as an obsessional neurosis. The interactions of fields and thinking are part of the interdisciplinary nature of academic life and are especially important for a subject as complex as religion. Some of these figures, like Durkheim, are important for more than one of our chapters.

Particularly in the early stages of many of the approaches under consideration, people claimed that they were being 'scientific'. This emphasis is there in the title *Introduction to the Science of Religion* (1873) by Friedrich Max Mueller (1823–1900 CE). What Mueller meant in his use of the term was that he was collecting, classifying and comparing materials, in his case textual material and examples of myths, much as a botanist or zoologist collects examples of species and sub-species. Other emphases in the use of the term scientific involve the claim that the exploration of religions does not involve commitment or belief and is rooted in human reason, rather than any appeal to revealed 'facts' or 'truths'; that it is systematic, objective, rational and based on evidence of some kind or another. Contemporarily we would distinguish between the methods and claim to be scientific of the natural sciences which have an emphasis on laboratory experiments which can be repeated and the social sciences, which use methods which are both *quantitative* (statistical analysis of social samples and questionnaires, for example) and *qualitative* (interviews and descriptive fieldwork, for example). But we would also now be realistic about the presuppositions involved in most academic investigations and scholarly stances and the imaginative leaps that are often involved in the formation of scientific hypotheses.

BIBLIOGRAPHY

Capps, Walter H. (1995), *Religious Studies: The Making of A Discipline*, Minneapolis: Fortress Press.
Hinnells, John R. (ed.) (2005), *The Routledge Companion to the Study of Religion*, Abingdon: Routledge.
McCutcheon, Russell (ed.) (1999), *The Insider Outsider Problem in The Study of Religion*, London: Cassell.
Sharpe, Eric [1975] (2nd ed. 1986), *Comparative Religion: A History*, London: Duckworth.

3. STUDY OF RELIGIONS AND THEOLOGY

There is no universal consensus as to what is the exact nature of either Christian Theology or Religious Studies.

Frank Whaling, 1986: 127

1. WHAT'S IN A NAME?

There are many different departments, schools and faculties in the United Kingdom with a particular focus on the study of religion and religions. What they are called is part of the history of that particular university and names are often retained for reasons of tradition, even when syllabuses and staffing have developed. For example, the name Divinity (Edinburgh and Cambridge) or Theology (Oxford, Nottingham and Exeter) derive from the time when the main focus of study was Christianity, the core of which was the study of the Bible (with the inclusion of learning Greek and Hebrew), Christian doctrines and Church history. But the syllabus in these places is now much wider. One department (Sheffield) is called specifically Biblical Studies and one (Heythrop) a Department of Systematic Theology. But you will also see that many have added the phrase 'Religious Studies' or a similar term to their original titles. So at the time of writing Aberdeen is Divinity and Religious Studies; Bristol, Glasgow and Leeds are Theology and Religious Studies; Birmingham and Cardiff are Religious and Theological Studies. Manchester is Religions and Theology; Lampeter is Theology, Religious Studies and Islamic Studies and at Oxford Brookes you can do a degree in Theology and Religion or in Religion, Culture and Ethics. The University of Gloucester department is called Religion, Culture and Philosophy and in

2004, Durham integrated the Religious Studies staff team from Newcastle to become a Department of Theology and Religion. There are other departments, too, that have not been listed and the details may change during the lifetime of this book.

The growth of Religious Studies or the Study of Religions in the UK owes much of its dynamism to the founding in 1967 of the first Department of Religious Studies in the University of Lancaster under the creative direction of Ninian Smart. Now, in addition to the extension of the names and work of the other departments, some of which are listed above, there are also departments of Religious Studies at the Open University; and at the School of Oriental and African Studies, University of London, and Bath Spa University College, where it is called The Study of Religions. Names are significant and there was a very definite philosophy of the field in its development in Lancaster, to which we shall return. But more important than titles alone are the syllabuses in the different departments and the range of methods and religions on which they focus. These you can see from prospectuses and you should also ask about courses that are to be offered at open days or if you go for an interview. Look at the lists of courses or modules available in prospectuses or on web sites to see what religions and styles of approach are studied at your prospective university.

After the points I have made above, you may ask why this guide was not given the longer title *Get Set for Theology and Religious Studies*. The reasons are twofold. Firstly, the subject at examination level in schools is usually called religious studies, so that is what is most familiar to you. Secondly, the phrase 'religious studies', or 'the study of religions', can claim to include theology or theologies. To begin to understand a little more about this second point, we need to ask what is meant by theology.

2. THE TERM 'THEOLOGY'

As with definitions of religion, answers to this question are varied and what follows is not exhaustive. You will be able to add other explanations on the basis of your conversations and reading.

The literal meaning of the term 'theology' derives from two Greek words: theos (God, gods or the divine) and logos (reflection on, or reasoned discourse about or study of). So, 'reflection on the being and nature of God, gods or the Divine' would be a good definition. It is a term whose usage historically and academically has been predominantly Christian and so the 'old' departments of Theology in the UK and further afield were concerned with thinking about God (and by association God's relationship with humans) from a Christian perspective. The enquiry traditionally was conducted by *insiders*, people who were themselves Christians, and one famous definition of theology is by Anselm (1033–1109 CE), who asserted 'I believe in order that I may understand'.

Theology is 'faith seeking understanding'.

Anselm, Archbishop of Canterbury (1033–1109 CE)

In modern university contexts, however, Christian Theology can be seen as the study of various Christians' explorations of their faith, as the history of Christian theologies. This is a second order rather than the first-order activity of Christians exploring their own faith, although it does not exclude that some students and staff may still be using the opportunity to do that. But there are no faith entry requirements for students and on the whole (with the exception of some Chairs of Theology still tied to Anglican ordination) no official credal tests for staff. This is especially the case where theology is taught in self-consciously secular universities.

At this point we may ask whether we can use the term 'theology' across religious traditions, since others, apart from Christians, have faith and believe in God or the Divine. The answer is 'yes', but with the following qualifications. Firstly, the word needs an adjective to make it clear what and whose explorations we are talking about. So any department which retains the term 'theology' in the traditional sense of focusing on

Christian teachings might call itself a Department of Christian Theology. Secondly, although there is Jewish, Muslim, Hindu and Sikh theological reflection, theology as the study of creed and belief (which it has traditionally been in Christianity) might not be the primary reflective exercise, the way of entry into studying their faiths for Muslims, Hindus and others. For example, it is argumentation about the meaning for practice and deed, of right action rather than right belief, that is the focus of the study of the *Talmud* and its interpretation of *Torah* in Jewish *yeshivahs*. It is the exploration of *Shar'ia* as a way of life based on the *Qur'an* and *Hadith* that is the primary concern of Muslim scholars in the *madrasas*. This does not mean that there are no Islamic or Jewish theologies, but that these are not traditionally the primary focus, 'style' or starting points of these faiths. Thirdly, Buddhists and *Advaita Vedanta* Hindus do not focus on a personal God (Theos) as their Ultimate Reality, so the term does not seem appropriate for them.

Those who are reluctant to abandon the word 'theology' without adjectives, seen as an overarching term, might suggest that 'theos' can be used in a very broad way to include a variety of religions, for example, as is intended in Rudolf Otto's use of the term 'The Holy'; Paul Tillich's exploration of what concerns a person ultimately or 'Ultimate Reality' and John Hick's 'The Real'. If a department says, as is suggested above, that their perspective for studying theology is inclusive and does not have confessionalist, insider Christian assumptions, or concentrate on Christianity alone, then investigate this claim by looking at the syllabus and the vocabulary that is used. Are the Jewish scriptures referred to as the 'Old Testament', the Christian, not Jewish, terminology for what Jews call The Law, Prophets and Writings or *Tenakh* and for which 'Jewish Scriptures' might be seen as a descriptive term (see Part I Chapter 2)? Is there also reference to 'non-Christian religions' instead of the use of a general phrase such as 'a variety of religions' or a listing of the exact names of the traditions being considered? If 'other religions' are studied, is the course about a) Christian approaches to or Christian theologies of other religions or b) explorations of other religions in their own terms independently of what Christians think of them? These are some of the different ways in which the study of religions might be included in a theology department's courses. Also look at the weighting of staff and their specialities. Here is a current definition from a Cambridge theologian who intends to use the term 'theology' in the broadest possible way:

> Theology at its broadest is thinking about questions raised by and about the religions.
>
> David Ford (1999)

> Wisdom is perhaps the most comprehensive and least controversial term for what theology is about. Wisdom may embrace describing, understanding, explaining, knowing and deciding, not only regarding matters of empirical fact but also regarding values, norms, beliefs and the shaping of lives, communities and institutions.
>
> David Ford (2005)

However, the approach of Ford's work, as he acknowledges himself, is from a Christian perspective.

The above issues, and others, have led to further developments in the widest possible sense in which the term 'theology' might be used, but ones that are still rooted in the traditional Christian definition of Anselm. An example of this is to see it as any *insiders*' explorations of their own traditions and what enables any religious practitioner to reflect on the truths of that tradition. So a recent book has the unusual title *Buddhist Theology* and adopts the definition of the American theologian David Tracy, who sees 'theology' as meaning the intellectual interpretations of any religious tradition from within, as long as the tradition conceives some notion of Ultimate Reality, which many would say is part of what it means to be a 'religion' rather than a secular worldview.

> The intellectual reflection within a religious tradition.
>
> David Tracy (1988)

The majority of these definitions and emphases seem to be on *insiders'* interpretations, including the study of, rather than the holding of, these *insiders'* views. Since even within a religion interpretations will be varied, the study of theologies can be seen as different from doing theology. Study is a second-order activity, hence the claim that that you do not have to be a Christian to study Christian theology, any more than you have to be religious to study religions. These points are part of the debate about the place of *insiders* and *outsiders* in the accurate understanding of any tradition (see also Part II Chapter 4).

3.   WHAT IS RELIGIOUS STUDIES?

Here is a comment by a Professor of Religion at the School of Oriental and African Studies, University of London.

> If you don't know the difference between theology and religious studies, then you're a theologian.
>
> Brian Bocking (1994)

One of the main differences that have been made historically between theology and religious studies, particularly as emphasised by those whose field is religious studies, is that no particular religious beliefs are necessary to study religions. Notice from the above that this is also now said of the study of theology. What is required is a rigorous intellectual interest in the issues and the material. This does not mean that people need to abandon their faith positions, but that those positions are not necessary for their understanding of elements of the course. In a contemporary department students might have any faith or none and the scholars whose work is examined and used and who have been important in the debates about the nature of religion and its roots may have denied the existence of an Ultimate Reality and been critical of religious beliefs and institutions. Examples of these are Marx and Freud, whose works may be as interesting for the student as key figures such as

Ramanuja or Nagarjuna, Maimonides, al-Ghazali or Aquinas, who are within the great traditions of Hinduism, Buddhism, Judaism, Islam and Christianity respectively and studied as part of them.

Studying a range of religions is not a new idea in the early twenty-first century. For example, as was mentioned in the Introduction to Part II, it was a concern of Friedrich Max Mueller in Oxford in the nineteenth century when he wrote an *Introduction to the Science of Religion* in 1873.

4. MAKING COMPARISONS IS NOT ESSENTIAL

Many still equate the study of religions with the term 'comparative religion' or 'comparative theology' and though being comparative may be an element in the field, the study of religions or religious studies encompasses much more and does not necessitate comparisons. An accurate study of a Buddhist text or a Sikh ceremony or a Jewish ethical idea does not require comparison for it to be properly understood, but does need to be located within the roundedness of its own context. Material should not be torn out of the holistic context of a tradition in a way that produces an inaccurate interpretation. For example, a ritual of prostration may not have the same implications and meaning for the Buddhist as for the Muslim and *monotheism* means different things in different contexts. Scholars who do make comparisons need to be careful that the intention of comparisons is not to assert the superiority of one tradition over another, for example, of the world religions over *indigenous* traditions, which used to be called *primitive* (see Part II Chapter 6). Comparing aspects of religions and theologies (see 'thematic comparisons' mentioned in section 5) may be an area within the study of religions for some, but the phrase 'comparative religion' is not a good overall description of the field, which is multidisciplinary and polymethodic (see section 5).

5. MAPPING THE FIELD

The importance in the UK of the founding of the new Lancaster Department of Religious Studies in 1967 was mentioned above. Ninian Smart, the founding Professor of that department and, some might say, of much in contemporary study of religions, suggested 'worldviews' as a wider term than 'religion' (see Part I Chapter 1). He saw religious studies as a multi-disciplinary field with a breadth and detachment from confessional bias which made it appropriate, interesting and relevant for the student in contemporary secular and plural societies and as a world citizen. Note that the third point and the sentence at the end of the list below include what can be called 'theologies' as described above. There is also an emphasis on structured empathy or sympathetic imagination, which are important in particular in the phenomenology of religion (see Part II Chapter 4).

First, it is plural, dealing with the many religions and secular worldviews of the globe.

Second, it is open-ended in the sense that it includes consideration of belief-systems and symbols lying beyond the frontiers of traditional religions.

Third, it treats worldviews both historically and systematically, and attempts to enter, through structured empathy, into the viewpoint of the believers.

Fourth, it makes thematic comparisons which help to illuminate the separate traditions.

Fifth, it is polymethodic: it uses many methods drawn from various disciplines – history, art history, philology, archeology, sociology, anthropology, philosophy and so on.

Sixth, it aims to show the power of religious ideas and practices and their interactions with other aspects of human existence.

Seventh, it can set the scene not only for an educated understanding of the world and its various belief-systems, but also for a personal quest for religious truth.

A central part is played in all this by the process of structured empathy. It is the way we cross our own horizons into the world of other people.

Ninian Smart (1995)

As well as the breadth of the methods employed within religious studies, which are well covered in this book, there is also a breadth in the range of aspects of religions that are considered. These are part of the many dimensions of religions now emphasised by most scholars and which highlight the fact that religions are about much more than just what people believe. So religious studies departments may include courses on social practice, rituals, the arts, spirituality, mythologies, gender issues and ethics, for example.

Another breadth which those involved in religious studies may emphasise is its usefulness in the modern world for a variety of professions. Knowing about a variety of religious traditions is beneficial in most walks of life from the social services, the police force, the leisure industry and international politics as well as teaching, for example. Not only are religions interesting in their own right, which is perhaps the best reason for wanting to study them, but this study can also make people truly global citizens.

The contemporary geo-political situation has changed so profoundly that the study of religions at all levels can only be carried out successfully if undertaken in a global perspective, given the need for more information, explanation and understanding at all levels of society.

Ursula King (1990), *Turning Points in Religious Studies*, Edinburgh: T. & T. Clark

BIBLIOGRAPHY

Bocking, Brian (1994), *The Teaching of Religion in Higher Education*, in Wiebe, Donald and Peter Masefield (eds) *Aspects of Religion*, New York: Peter Lang.

Braun, Willi and Russell T. McCutcheon (2000), *Guide to The Study of Religion*, London: Cassell.

Ford, David (1999), *Theology: A Very Short Introduction*, Oxford: Oxford University Press.

Ford, David (2005), *Theology* in John R. Hinnells (ed.) *The Routledge Companion to The Study of Religion*, Abingdon: Routledge.

Jackson, Roger and John Makransky (eds) (2000), *Buddhist Theology: Critical Reflections by Contemporary Buddhist Scholars*, Richmond: Curzon.

Jacobs, Louis (1973), *Jewish Theology*, London: Darton, Longman and Todd.

King, Ursula (1990), *Turning Points in Religious Studies*, Edinburgh: T. & T. Clark.

Smart, Ninian [1983] (2nd ed. 1995), *Worldviews*, New Jersey: Prentice Hall.

Tracy, David (1988), *Comparative Theology* in Mircea Eliade (ed.) *Encyclopedia of Religion*, New York: Macmillan Vol. 14 pp. 446–55.

Watt, W. Montgomery (1985), *Islamic Philosophy and Theology*, Edinburgh: Edinburgh University Press.

Whaling, Frank (1986), *Christian Theology and World Religions*, Basingstoke: Marshall Pickering.

4. STUDY OF RELIGIONS AND PHENOMENOLOGY

1. INTRODUCTION

'Phenomenology' may well be the word amongst all those in our headings that sounds the most unfamiliar and complicated. It is, like so many of the other terms we have used, derived from the Greek and can be translated literally as 'reflection on that which appears'. It seeks to answer the question of how we understand and interpret (*hermeneutics*) religion and religions. The sections below attempt to clarify what is involved in the use of the term in three overlapping ways: phenomenology as a distinctive style of approach; phenomenology as an accumulation of conventions; and key figures in the development of phenomenology of religion. As can also be said for other perspectives, it is not just one single, rigorous method and systematic discipline, but much more an accumulation of conventions introduced and used with differing emphases by different scholars. The central challenge for all our perspectives is one of understanding, and the central question is how we can understand the religions of those different from ourselves and what is involved in that act of understanding, for which the technical term is *verstehen*. Phenomenologists have their own ways of responding to this challenge, which can be expressed in the saying of the *indigenous* people of North America: 'never judge a person until you have walked a mile in their moccassins' (see Part I Chapter 1) and in the following quotation from Harper Lee's novel *To Kill a Mockingbird* (1962):

> Atticus stood up and walked to the end of the porch. When he completed his first examination of the wisteria vine he strolled back to me.

'First of all,' he said, 'if you can learn a simple trick, Scout, you'll get along a lot better with all kinds of folks. You never really understand a person until you consider things from his point of view –'

'Sir?'

– 'until you climb into his skin and walk around in it'.

The first section that follows deals with what seems to be the main emphasis of the phenomenological approach to religion and religions. The next section develops some of the key terms which scholars have used and which constitute key elements in their approaches. Finally, we shall introduce some of the key figures in the historical development of phenomenology of religions. As we pointed out in the general introduction to this whole section, each perspective we have identified as important for the study of religions includes a variety of approaches, hence the use of the plural 'phenomenologies and phenomenologists'.

2. PHENOMENOLOGY AS A DISTINCTIVE STYLE OF APPROACH

Phenomenology involves an approach to religion and religions which takes full account of the *insiders*', the believers' and the belongers' understandings of their traditions. It consists of trying to understand religions in their own terms, from the point of view of those whose religions they are. I use both 'believer' and 'belonger' here because many religions are not focused primarily on beliefs (see Part I Chapter 1). That point in itself reflects a phenomenological approach. Whether phenomenologists are writing and teaching about one religion or various religions, they are not interested in presenting a picture that would not ring true to *insiders*. They want to make the subject of study speak with its own authentic voice, to imaginatively enter into worldviews different from their own.

The Norwegian phenomenologist who worked in Holland, W. Brede Kristenson (1867–1953 CE), made the intriguing statement 'the believer is always right' in his book *The Meaning of Religion* [1954] (tr. 1960). This assertion is easy to misunderstand. It is not an endorsement of any or all of the actions or beliefs of religious people whatever those actions and beliefs are, but an assertion that the believers'/belongers' understanding of their tradition, their explanation of what they do and believe rather than an outside and possibly *reductionist* interpretation, is the one on which we need to concentrate and with which we should work. Kristenson says:

> Let us never forget that there exists no other religious reality than the faith of the believer. If we really want to understand religion, we must refer exclusively to the believer's testimony . . . if our opinion about another religion differs from the opinion and evaluation of the believers, then we are no longer talking about their religion. We have turned aside from historical reality and are concerned only with ourselves.

(translated in Sharpe, 1986: 228)

Any mention of believers/belongers brings with it the knowledge that insiders are varied in an enormous number of ways, and that it is necessary to reflect variety in any description that is given. For example, neither the experience of worship nor pilgrimage are the same amongst all Muslims, let alone in all religions. The English term 'God' does not mean the same for everyone, even within any one religion. *Shi'a* Muslims have a particular understanding of the importance of the battle of Kerbala in early Islamic history which is different from that of *Sunnis*. *Mahayana* Buddhists understand the place of Gautama *Buddha* in their tradition differently from *Theravadins*. *Protestant* and *Eastern Orthodox* Christians have a different view of the place of the *Pope* from *Roman Catholics*. Perceiving the varieties of believers'/belongers' experiences and actions leads to an understanding that there is no such monolithic entity as 'Judaism', 'Buddhism' and so on (see Part I Chapter 2).

It is obvious that to understand what the beliefs and practices of religions mean to members of those religions we need to read books that are written by, for example, Buddhists and Sikhs as well as by scholars using the methods and skills of historians and anthropologists. These ways of studying are not mutually exclusive, as there are many Muslims and Hindus and others who are scholars as well as believers. Equally, there are good historians and anthropologists who empathise with their subject and evoke the worldviews about which they write. For this empathetic style of study, it is important to meet members of religious traditions as well as to read about them in books so that you can explore the variety of faiths and the place of these faiths in people's lives.

The attempt at understanding that is central to phenomenology involves exercising certain skills and working within certain conventions, which are outlined in the next section.

3.   PHENOMENOLOGY AS AN ACCUMULATION OF CONVENTIONS

Part II Chapter 3 included a quotation from Ninian Smart, who worked as a phenomenologist of religion and wrote both on one religion in *The Phenomenon of Christianity* and on a variety of religious traditions in *The World's Religions*. The quotation emphasised structured empathy and sympathetic imagination as important for the study of religions and that this is the way that 'we cross our own horizons into the world of other people'. An emphasis on these skills is not unique to phenomenology of religion, as can be seen from Part II Chapter 6 and the anthropologists' emphasis on fieldwork and also in sociologists' use of participant observation (see Part II Chapter 7). The key ideas that highlight phenomenologists' attempts to 'cross over' are listed below and overlap each other:

1. This style of study involves the capacity **to cross cultural distance** in understanding the faith of other people. The challenge to understand from within is also part of the study of history, anthropology and literature, for example.

2. A further important term is **empathy**, which refers in an additional way to our capacity to enter into another's worldview.

3. Sympathetic imagination and **evocation** are also important skills in this process towards understanding.

4. **Distancing** from one's own position is required. This is important as a first step in any academic study, whether it is history or work on a language where the alphabet and constructs may be quite different from one's own.

5. *Epoché*, another Greek word, is the 'bracketing out' or 'holding back' of one's own attitudes and value judgements, that is the suspension of value judgements and the setting aside of presuppositions. It is important to note, however, that these have to be recognised before they can be set aside. They are not necessarily obvious until one begins to engage in study, so the enterprise is ongoing, not just something one 'sorts out' before one begins. People also argue, quite rightly, about whether this is possible. Here it is set out as a desirable, though contested, goal, without any simplistic idea that it is easy or possible for everyone.

6. The observer's capacity to see the essentials in or essence of a situation or the material under study is what is known as *eidetic vision*. The root of the phrase is the Greek word 'eidos' which means 'essence'.

James Cox (1996), summarising Edmund Husserl (1859–1938 CE), outlines phenomenological method in the following steps:

- Suspend judgements, bracket previous theories, opinions, ideas or thoughts

- Disregard prior distinctions between the real or apparent, true or false

- Allow the phenomena to speak for themselves within the bracketed consciousness

- Build structures of meaning by naming objects, noting relationships and describing processes within the phenomena
- Intuit the essential meanings of the phenomena from their structures
- Test the intuition by going back to the phenomena, making adjustments where necessary

These emphases are related to two other key terms, *emic* and *etic*, which are most often used in anthropology today (see Part II Chapter 6) and show how interlinked methods can be.

> The *emic* perspective, then, is the outsider's attempt to produce as faithfully as possible – in a word to describe – the informant's own descriptions or productions of sounds, behavior, beliefs, etc. The *etic* perspective is the observer's subsequent attempt to take the descriptive information they have already gathered and to organize, systematize, compare – in a word – redescribe – the information in terms of a system of their own making.
>
> McCutcheon, 1999: 17

4. KEY FIGURES IN THE DEVELOPMENT OF PHENOMENOLOGY OF RELIGION

One way of understanding phenomenology of religion is to trace the use of the term, and other key words associated with it, in the work of key thinkers, some of whom we have already mentioned. The term was used in philosophy generally before it was applied to the study of religions. The work of the philosophers Immanuel Kant (1724–1804 CE) and Edmund Husserl are important here. Kant explored how we know about things (*epistemology*) and distinguished between what we can know in our everyday experience, things as they appear to us (phenomena) and things as they are in themselves (noumena) which are unknowable to us. Husserl provided future phenomenologists with key terms such as *epoché* and *eidetic vision*.

In 1887 Chantepie de la Saussaye (1848–1920 CE) coined the phrase 'phenomenology of religion' in his *Handbook of the History of Religion*, in which he groups together religious phenomena under themes, for example objects of worship, gods, holy places or scriptures. This kind of collection of material across religions has come to be called 'descriptive phenomenology' and has continued, with additional perspectives, in the work of some later phenomenologists such as Gerardus Van der Leeuw (1890–1950 CE), who writes about outward and inward actions and different types of religions and their founders, and Mircea Eliade (1907–86 CE), who writes about the elemental, timeless patterns of religious life. Van der Leeuw sees the task of the phenomenologist in five stages:

- To assign names to groups of phenomena – such as sacrifice, prayer, saviour, myth

- To interpolate the experiences within one's own life and experience them systematically

- To exercise *epoché* to withdraw to one side and observe

- To clarify and comprehend

- To confront chaotic reality and testify to what has been understood

5. QUESTIONING A METHOD

With any of the approaches that we are considering there will be questions and criticisms. In relationship to the work of phenomenologists, one of these is whether anyone can be truly objective and empathetic in relation to others' beliefs and practices, whether it is possible to 'climb into his skin and walk around in it'. These are educational and intellectual ideals which are worth trying to attain, but with a knowledge of our own limitations. These limitations are present in the work of scholars such as Van der Leeuw, who often evaluates the material he is describing, for example in his lack of sympathy for glossalalia (speaking in tongues), which he calls 'nothing more than verbosity' (Van der Leeuw, 1963: Section 3).

The assumption of many phenomenologists such as Eliade that we are homo religiosus – that the human is a religious being – is also more a theological belief and assertion than is often acknowledged and is itself a faith position. There is also a tendency amongst phenomenologists to see an essence in religion and religions, which seems to diminish and oversimplify the infinite varieties there are. Then we need to ask whether the thematic material that occurs so often in phenomenological works is taken out of the specific contexts of the histories and lived realities of individual religions. Some have also said that phenomenology is 'mere description', but as the following quotation suggests, there is nothing 'mere' about accurate description, which is the phenomenologists' aim.

> It is necessary to remember that description, in the sense of accurate judgement-free reporting, is invaluable in the study of religions.
>
> Marion Bowman in Sutcliffe (ed.) 2004: 3

Now that many scholars think that we have moved beyond the classical emphases of phenomenology of religions, there is more emphasis on the need for scholars to 'declare their perspective' in approaching any material and to acknowledge that their descriptions will be coloured by their own ethnicity, gender and worldview. Understanding can be seen to come through a dialogue of differences rather than through empathetic identification. However, the heart of the phenomenologist's enterprise, whatever it is called and whether it takes place in anthropology, sociology or historical studies, remains valuable. It challenges those who seek to reduce religion to some other aspect of human life and take a projectionist stance. It tries to seek out the categories appropriate to cultures and religions rather than describe them in terms that are alien to them and seeks to understand religions from *insiders*' viewpoints in order to engage in creative conversation.

BIBLIOGRAPHY

Cox, James (1996), *Expressing The Sacred*, Edinburgh: Edinburgh University Press.

Eliade, Mircea [1957] (tr. 1959), *The Sacred and The Profane*, New York: Harcourt, Brace & Co.

Flood, Gavin (1999), *Beyond Phenomenology*, London: Cassell.

McCutcheon, Russell T. (ed.) (1999), *The Insider/Outsider Problem in the Study of Religion*, London: Cassell.

Smart, Ninian (1973), *The Phenomenon of Religion*, New York: Herder and Herder.

Smart, Ninian (1979), *The Phenomenon of Christianity*, London: Collins.

Sutcliffe, Steven (ed.) (2004), *Religion: Empirical Studies*, Aldershot: Ashgate.

Van der Leeuw, Gerardus [1933 tr. 1938] (1963 ed.), *Religion in Essence and Manifestation*, New York: Harper.

5. STUDY OF RELIGIONS AND PHILOSOPHY

1. INTRODUCTION

The philosophy of religion as it is taught in the UK has focused primarily on issues that arise in relation to Christianity. This is quite natural as the history of universities and of philosophy itself are entwined with the history of Christian institutions and doctrines. Recent scholars of religion, such as Ninian Smart (1927–2001 CE), have broadened our understanding of the philosophy of religion. Every one of the world's religions, Smart notes, has philosophical aspects (this corresponds to Smart's 'doctrinal and philosophical dimension' of religions and also to Eric Sharpe's (1933–2000 CE) 'ethical mode' or 'function' of religion – see Part I Chapter 1). Contemporary writers such as John Hick and Keith Ward also work from a broad philosophy of religion background and the philosopher David Cooper engages with world, not just western, philosophies.

A comprehensive study of the philosophies of the world's religions would, however, require an encyclopedia. Nevertheless, it is worth remembering that your study of religions will involve some philosophical explorations. Sometimes you will find philosophies of different world religions that are similar to traditional Christian philosophy of religion. For example, Islamic arguments for the existence of God are similar to Christian arguments. Equally, sometimes you will find quite different philosophical traditions. The Buddhist philosophy of interdependence, examined in the *Avatamsaka Sutra*, of each and every part of the Universe being contained within and reflected by each and every other part is very different from Christian philosophy; you might recognise, however, that it is quite similar to modern ideas of *holo-*

graphy. Wherever there are religions there will always be simple and fundamental philosophical questions: is there an Ultimate Reality or God? What kind of 'person' is God? There are many questions about the existence of God, gods or the Real, and questions about the nature, or attributes, of that existence.

In this section we have concentrated on the kinds of questions and issues you will find most commonly in books and courses on the Philosophy of Religion in the UK. You might enquire of any department whether they offer courses which look at philosophies of religion that are more distinctly Islamic, Indian, Chinese or Buddhist, for example.

2.   ARGUMENTS FOR THE EXISTENCE OF GOD

There are four classic arguments for the existence of God. They are sometimes referred to as 'natural theology'. Many philosophers throughout history have offered strong refutations to these arguments, and there are equally many modern variants of them:

1. **The ontological argument:** The main form of this argument was developed by Anselm of Canterbury (1033–1109 CE). He stated that God necessarily exists because He is 'that than which nothing greater can be conceived'. He must exist, Anselm argued, because the greatest thing that can be conceived to exist must do so both in our understanding and in reality.

2. **The cosmological argument:** This argument answers the simple question: why are we here? Thomas Aquinas (1224–75 CE) examined the idea that everything has been caused by something else so there must be a 'first cause'. He defined God as that first cause. This style of reasoning was also used by the Jewish scholar Maimonides (1135–1204 CE) and the Muslim scholar Avicenna (Ibn Sina 980–1037 CE).

3. **The argument from design:** This argument grows out of the observation that the world is so beautiful and well ordered it cannot be the result of chance: it must be designed. William Paley (1743–1805 CE), who compared the design of the world to a watch, offered the most famous example of the design idea. God therefore becomes the 'watchmaker'.

4. **The moral argument:** Immanuel Kant (1724–1804 CE) suggested that the existence of moral laws and the human sense of duty offered a practical argument for the existence of God. For Kant, human free will to choose moral actions makes room for a God who has established a fixed moral order where humans can choose to act in good and evil ways.

3.   THE PROBLEM OF EVIL

A child who reflects on the existence and nature of God will quickly raise the objection: 'if there is a God, why does He allow bad things to happen?' The philosophical response to this question usually divides 'bad things' into two categories. There are natural disasters, such as the Asian tsunami of 2004, which even atheist insurers still euphemistically refer to as 'acts of God'; and there are human acts which cause suffering, such as rape, torture, paedophilia or murder. The area of philosophy that deals with the problem of God's justice and evil is called *theodicy*. *Theodicy* examines the way theology responds to the existence of evil in a world said to be created by a just, loving and all-powerful God.

Our example child, on studying Nazi Germany at school, will ask exactly the same question as theologians and philosophers of religion: 'What kind of God allows Auschwitz and the Final Solution to occur?' It is a question asked by many Jews also; and for some the response was that this event was proof for the non-existence of God. The philosopher of religion may further question three of the traditional attributes of God: God is good; God is all-knowing (*omniscient*); God is all-powerful (*omnipotent*). Given the existence of evil, each of these attributes can be challenged. For example, in relation to the creation of the world, we might ask:

1. If God is good how can He have created a world in which there is evil?

2. If God is omniscient why did He create a world in which He knew there would be evil?

3. If God is omnipotent why does He not create a world which is free of evil?

The primary response of philosophers from Augustine of Hippo (354–430 CE) to the contemporary scholar Richard Swinburne to these questions lies in free will. It is by the use of free will that humans have created evil and it is by free will that humans can choose to act in morally good ways (see Kant's moral argument for the existence of God). Muslim philosophers such as al-Ghazali (1058–1111 CE) have also examined the issue of free will.

4. THE PHILOSOPHY OF RELIGION AND PHILOSOPHY OF LANGUAGE

In the twentieth and twenty-first centuries Western philosophers have increasingly concentrated on the role of language in the way we understand the world. At the most basic level they have made clear that the concepts contained in the words of our language construct and constrict our understanding of the world. This is just as much the case in religion as in any other area of knowledge. So, philosophers of religion such as Anthony Flew and D. Z. Phillips have focused their studies on religious language, what it means and how it is used by believers.

Perhaps the most influential philosopher of recent times is Ludwig Wittgenstein (1889–1951 CE). His concept of

'language games' has been one of the most widely used in
philosophy of religion (see box on p. 70). Religious language
operates within its own game, with its own rules. From the
perspective of those sympathetic to religion this means religious language cannot be judged as true or false by the rules
of another language game, such as science. Yet from another
perspective this reduces religious language to merely one
game amongst others. God and faith then become very
limited functions of a humanly constructed language.

5.   THE PHILOSOPHICAL DEATH OF GOD

Friedrich Nietzsche (1844–1900 CE) famously declared, 'God
is dead'. His proclamation is important in the philosophy of
religion because it points us towards a number of philosophical and other challenges to the existence of religion in the last
two centuries.

- Philosophically – arguments for the existence of God have
  become less interesting to philosophers in general. Kant
  showed that, other than in the moral argument, the assumption that God exists could not be sustained. Furthermore,
  Ludwig Feuerbach (1804–72 CE) showed that the human
  concept of God could be defined as a projection of human
  desires onto the world.

- Psychologically – psychologists such as Sigmund Freud
  (1856–1939 CE) would go further and suggest the idea of
  God and religion itself is a 'universal obsessional neurosis'
  (see also Part II Chapter 8).

- Scientifically – Charles Darwin's (1809–82 CE) theory of
  evolution in *The Origin of Species* (1869) undermined the
  history of creation as defined by Christianity. Scientists from
  the nineteenth century on increasingly realised they did not
  need God in their theories. And the burden of proof for what
  were once commonly accepted as miracles meant other
  explanations such as chance or natural causes could explain

God's action in the world. The engagement of philosophers of religion, theologians and scientists is still a thriving area of debate.

- Sociologically – with the decreasing need for religion as an explanation for why the world is as it is, people in the modern industrialised world became more *secular*. The process of *secularisation*, in the way people understand the world and in the way religion influences people's daily lives, began in the nineteenth century and continues in the UK today (see also Part II Chapter 7).

Philosophy of religion remains a vital element in the study of religions and of philosophy in general. You might wonder why this is so when the world appears to be increasingly secular in orientation. Yet interest in religion remains vibrant. There are a number of reasons for this. Feminist philosophers of religion have pointed out that the masculine 'God' is very much a part of male-dominated societies and ways of seeing the world. There is a growth in ideas of the female attributes of God in many religions, and religions such as *Paganism* that revere *goddesses*. The modern globalised world has increased movement of religious and ethnic groups so there are a great variety of religions practised in the UK today with significant numbers of followers. Equally, there is a growth in new and alternative forms of religion or ways of practising religion, in part influenced by the world's religions. Furthermore, a number of scholars are pointing out that belief in religious ideas and the idea of God has declined only a little in the last two centuries, despite the decline in belonging to a religious institution (see Part II Chapter 7). Finally, the fundamental questions about the meaning of life, the challenge of suffering and death and the existence of spirits, powers or gods do not change, though the answers to them do.

Wittgenstein and the study of religion

The philosopher of language Ludwig Wittgenstein suggested that there are many forms of language, which he called 'language games'. Wittgenstein said there is no single language with a single set of rules or meanings. A language game is one part of a whole collection of different ways of describing the world. So poetry, science and religion are all different language games; they are, however, related. They share words, concepts and meanings. The important thing to remember for Wittgenstein is that words gain meaning from their context, that is from the way they are used. So religious statements about God's creation of the world or the power of prayer may not make sense in a scientific explanation for the creation of the world or why things happen, but they do make sense in the language of religion.

Another Wittgensteinian idea commonly used in the study of religions is the idea of 'family resemblances'. Certain concepts, such as the word 'game' itself, include activities that seem to share few similarities, such as the games of chess and football. They are linked, Wittgenstein suggested, through other games that share similarities with both. So chess is similar to other two-person competitive games that share similarities with other competitive team games like football. Thus football and chess are 'related'. They share what Wittgenstein called 'family resemblances'. The same is true of religions. Daoism and Judaism, for example, share few similarities, yet are linked by other religions that do share some family resemblances. The family resemblance model groups religions according to close family groups. So Judaism, Christianity and Islam may be grouped as Abrahamic or Semitic traditions while Hinduism, Sikhism, Jainism and Buddhism may be grouped as Indian traditions.

BIBLIOGRAPHY

Anderson, Pamela Sue (1998), *A Feminist Philosophy of Religion*, Oxford: Blackwell.

Bowker, John (2005), *Sacred Neuron: Extraordinary New Discoveries Linking Science and Religion*, London: I. B. Tauris.

Burnham, Douglas (2003), *Get Set for Philosophy*, Edinburgh: Edinburgh University Press.

Clack, Beverley and Brian Clack (1988), *The Philosophy of Religion: A Critical Introduction*, London: Polity.

Cooper, David (1996), *World Philosophies: An Historical Introduction*, Oxford: Blackwell.

Davies, Brian (1993), *An Introduction to the Philosophy of Religion*, Oxford: Oxford University Press.

Fisher, Rob (1999), 'Philosophical Approaches' in P. Connolly (ed.) *Approaches to the Study of Religion*, London: Cassell, 105–34.

Smart, Ninian (1999), *World Philosophies*, London: Routledge.

Swinburne, Richard (1991), *The Existence of God*, Oxford: Clarendon Press.

6. STUDY OF RELIGIONS AND ANTHROPOLOGY

1. INTRODUCTION

The word 'anthropology', again from Greek roots, is usually translated as 'the study of humankind'. The study of humankind could be the study of the physical structure of human beings, of their skeletons, as in biological anthropology, so the term anthropology needs an adjective to indicate exactly what kind of study is being discussed. Just as there are different sorts of theologians, mathematicians, geographers and historians, so there are different sorts of anthropologists. The kinds of anthropology which we shall explore are cultural and social anthropologies, and their concerns and methods, which include *ethnography*, overlap a great deal with both sociology and phenomenology. There is even further variety, because some scholars are more interested in the function and some in the structures of religion in societies, for example. One difficulty for anthropologists is separating out what is called 'religion' from other aspects of human life. Michael Gilsenan says in his book *Recognising Islam* that the topics and themes with which he deals:

> Do not appear at first glance to have much to do with Islam or religion: the furnishing of the salon of the Lebanese bourgeoisie; sexuality, honour and violation linked to God's grace, the street plan of modern Cairo; tribal markets; family feuds, genealogies and so forth.

> Gilsenan, 1982: 19

This is a reminder of the emphasis on Islam and other religious traditions as 'ways of life' that was explored in Part I Chapter 1. This emphasis has led many anthropologists to offer their own definitions which do not separate something called religion from other aspects of societies, cultures, ways of living and viewing the world.

Anthropology as a discipline dates from the late nineteenth century when there was considerable interest in finding the origins of humankind, which included attempts to find the origins of religion in what were then called *primitive* religions and societies. These were placed on an evolutionary ladder and seen as the earliest examples of religions and at the origins of what had now evolved to a more advanced and rational stage, which to some was superceded in the worldview associated with *science*. The terms 'primal' or 'tribal' and even 'savage' as well as '*primitive*' were applied to these societies and their religions to distinguish them from developed 'civilisations' and the so-called 'great' or 'world' religions. Contemporary scholars reject an evolutionist view and the term now used for these formerly-called *primitive* ways of life is *indigenous* traditions and the polarisation with other sorts of religious beliefs and practices is not made so strongly today.

2. CENTRAL CONCERNS

In her introduction to *The Anthropology of Religion*, Fiona Bowie sets out a series of questions which highlight many of the general concerns of anthropologists, while pointing out that they concern those in other disciplines, too. This is why there is so often an emphasis on the need for the study of religions to be interdisciplinary or multidisciplinary (see the Introduction to Part I).

> In studying human society we are looking at both ourselves and others, and the dialectical relationship between self and other, the individual and the group, lies at the heart of anthropology. Who is this 'other'? And what can the other tell us about ourselves, our culture, our society? Are the others human? And what does this mean? Do small-scale 'primitive' societies mirror the evolutionary past of the 'civilised' world? What, if any, are the underlying

similarities between peoples? Are we all so different that each culture and society can only be looked at in isolation – with little or no basis for comparison? Is religion merely a product of society, merely human invention and projection? Or is there 'more in heaven and earth' than the material or social scientist can explain?

Bowie, 2000: 1

Another way of emphasising the central concerns of anthroplogists and why their contribution to the study of religions is so valuable is articulated in the following extract from a book review. The review is of a novel about India by Heather Wood called *Third Class Ticket*, which the reviewer, who has himself worked as an anthropologist, sees as a new genre of 'anthropological novel' parallel to the genre of 'historical novel'.

At the heart of anthropology lies an ambivalence which puzzles, frustrates and even disenchants many of its students. Is it an art or a science? Many take up the subject because of a curiosity about human beings and their relationships, a wish to learn how people differently circumstanced differ from us and to what extent they are still like us, an urge to extend the limits of their own imaginative experience. Such anthropologists, who aspire above all to empathize and sympathize . . . have been called philanthropologists. They might have studied literature or history, but a spirit of adventure has made them want to see for themselves and directly to experience life under conditions remote from those of their upbringing. This experience of fieldwork they share with those driven by more purely intellectual motives, whose explorations are designed to formulate and test hypotheses about the behaviour of men in society. The two motivations may indeed be united in a single breast, and the most inspiring works of anthropology are fruits of such a union. But some philanthropologists feel, while collecting genealogies or trying to order their field notes into theses, that they have strayed into the wrong game, and that they would do more justice to themselves and their subjects if they could only distill their experiences into a novel . . . had they but the talent.

Richard Gombrich in *Journal of The Oxford University India Society* Vol. 1 No. 1, May 1980

You will notice how much that is said in this review resonates with terms such as 'sympathetic imagination' and 'empathy'; 'self and other'; 'insider and outsider' that are a focus in the discussion of phenomenology and sociology (see Part II Chapters 4 and 7). This again illustrates how difficult it is to separate in a rigid way the approaches that contribute to the study of religions.

Another way of seeing the distinctive interests of anthropologists is to contrast some of their emphases and methods with those of scholars who developed abstract theories about societies and with those of historians and textual scholars. David Gellner comments:

> Close study of particular societies was to suggest that explaining everything in terms of some grand historical design was hardly the way to understand a living society.
>
> Gellner, 1999: 16

The chart below suggests some further contrasts, using illustrations from the study of Hinduism:

Historians and Textual Scholars	Anthropologists
the 'great tradition' of a religion	the 'little traditions'
a unity: e.g. Hinduism	varieties: e.g. village Hinduisms Divali in Leicester
classical texts: e.g. Vedas	local contexts
written literature	oral traditions
classical languages: e.g. Sanskrit	vernacular languages: e.g. Gujerati Bengali Hindi
publicly held beliefs	local and individual beliefs
official orthodox normative	popular accretive actual
historical accumulation	cultural variety contemporary groups

The study of life in a variety of Hindu villages may challenge the whole monolithic category of 'Hinduism', just as comparisons of Christian beliefs and practices in a Brazilian and an English village may challenge the unitive category of 'Christianity'. Having separated out and increased awareness of the differences in these emphases, many anthropologists may also try to relate their particular studies to the classical, textual and historical dimensions of the societies on which they work. Richard Gombrich does this in his examination of Buddhism in Sri Lanka entitled *Precept and Practice* (1971). Clifford Geertz in his *Islam Observed* (1968), later published as *After The Fact: Two Countries, Four Decades, One Anthropologist* (1995), compares the differences between Islamic life in Morocco and Indonesia in different historical periods, whilst emphasising that:

> The anthropologist is always inclined to turn towards the concrete, the particular, the microscopic. We are the miniaturists of the social sciences, painting on lilliputian canvases with what we take to be delicate strokes. We hope to find in the little what eludes us in the large, to stumble upon general truths while sorting through special cases.
>
> Geertz [1968], 1995

There are also certain themes which have been the focus of attention in anthropological studies. Fiona Bowie identifies these as: the place of symbols, particularly that of the body; the making of boundaries and construction of identities; sex and gender; culture and environment; ritual; shamanism and witchcraft. We shall return to some of these themes in Part II Chapter 9.

3. THE IMPORTANCE OF FIELDWORK

In order to present their studies, anthropologists have to complete accurate first-hand fieldwork on which their descriptions are based. There was a time when 'other' societies were described by so-called 'armchair' anthropologists (for example, Durkheim, in his work on the Australian aborigines), who based their descriptions on the work of missionaries, travellers, civil servants and those who wrote diaries and letters about the peoples amongst whom they were living or met on their journey. Even when anthropologists first travelled to the places about which they wanted to write, they lived slightly separately from the peoples they were studying, looking down, as it were, from their verandas onto the activities of a village and using interpreters to ask their questions and tell them the meaning of the answers, and describe the activities of the people. Now anthropologists are expected to learn the vernacular languages of the communities they study and to live amongst them in as inclusive a way as possible, meticulously recording everything they see and hear. However, there is always debate about the difference the presence of any stranger, even the most empathetic and integrated person, will make to a situation and contemporary anthropologists try to be as open as possible about their own interests and assumptions and how these are reflected in the questions they ask and the answers they receive. There are also those who use their own agendas of interest positively, such as the *feminist* anthropologists who have focused on the place and roles of women in different societies.

Key terms linked to the changes of emphasis in anthropological method outlined above are *etic* and *emic*. An *etic* approach involves looking at cultures from the outside, from the viewpoint of various universal categories and theories (see Gellner's comment above), which is what the early anthropologists and some sociologists did. The *emic* emphasises the exploration of the categories used by the insiders themselves and being able to interpret events as a cultural whole in the way that the people themselves do. The kind of description that is seen as appropriate is called 'thick' description.

4. SOME KEY FIGURES IN THE ANTHROPOLOGY OF RELIGION

Sir Edward Burnett Tylor (1832–1917 CE) held the first official university post in anthropology in Britain when in 1884 he became Reader in Anthropology at Oxford University. His most famous book is *Primitive Culture*, published in 1871, in which he defines religion as 'belief in spiritual beings' and sees cultures as evolving from *animism* (which he defined as the *primitive* belief that there is a life-force, anima, in everything) to *polytheism* (belief in many gods) to *monotheism* (belief in one God).

The Cambridge anthropologist Sir James Frazer (1854–1951 CE) had a background in classics and put together a massive collection of examples of *myths*, *legends*, beliefs and practices in his famous *The Golden Bough* (1890). His examples, taken out of the context of the societies in which they were originally embedded, demonstrated an evolution from belief in the power of *magic* to a dependence on religion and then the development of *science* as a way of understanding the world.

Emile Durkheim (1858–1917 CE) is an equally important figure in the development of sociology as anthropology. His most important book (written in his native French in 1912 and translated into English in 1915) is *The Elementary Forms of the Religious Life* in which he concentrates on religion as a social system. He wanted to find the main elements of religion and his emphasis is on the function of religion in societies. One of his key distinctions is between the sacred and the profane, which he suggested all religions presuppose. He examines (through secondary sources) the life of the Australian aborigines in which he sees the fundamental elements of religion and society in general. His definition of religion is that it is 'a unified system of beliefs and practices relative to sacred things, that is, things set apart and forbidden'. The distinction between sacred and profane is also important in the work of the British anthropologist Mary Douglas, whose analysis of the concepts in the biblical text, especially Leviticus, have been very influential. She develops her ideas in her book *Purity and Danger* (1966).

Bronislaw Malinowski (1884–1942 CE) was a Pole who worked in Britain and, along with the German Franz Boas (1858–1942 CE), who worked in the USA, developed detailed field studies. Malinowski completed pioneering fieldwork for two years in the Trobriand Islands off Papua New Guinea where he learned the language of the people, recorded what he saw and heard and saw practices and ideas as fulfilling a function for peoples within their whole society and fulfilling real needs. He saw religion as a psychological support in the face of death, and a binding force in society. His method came to be called 'participant observation' and has been since his time the central method in anthropology.

The American anthropologist Clifford Geertz has written about religion as a cultural system in his *The Interpretation of Cultures* (1973). He advocates what has come to be called an interpretive approach which emphasises presenting things from the point of view of the people themselves, presenting their understanding of the meaning of what they are doing and letting the research agenda emerge from the context. The description is *emic* (insider) and 'thick'.

BIBLIOGRAPHY

Bowie, Fiona (2000), *The Anthropology of Religion*, Oxford: Blackwell.

Fuller, C.J. (1992), *The Camphor Flame: Popular Hinduism and Society in India*, Princeton: Princeton University Press.

Geertz, Clifford (1973), *The Interpretation of Cultures*, New York: Basic Books.

Geertz, Clifford [1971 as *Islam Observed*] (1995), *After The Fact: Two Countries, Four Decades, One Anthropologist*, Cambridge, MA: Harvard University Press.

Gilsenan, Michael (1982), *Recognising Islam: Islam and Society in the Modern Middle East*, London: Croom Helm.

Gombrich, Richard (1971), *Precept and Practice*, Oxford: Clarendon Press.

Harvey, Graham (ed.) (1999), *Indigenous Religions: A Companion*, London: Cassell.

James, Wendy and Douglas H. Johnson (eds) (1988), *Vernacular Christianity*, Oxford: JASO.

Lambek, Michael (ed.) (2001), *A Reader in the Anthropology of Religion*, Oxford: Blackwell.

Spiro, Melford (1970), *Buddhism and Society*, Berkeley: University of California Press.

Wood, Heather (1980), *Third Class Ticket*, London: Penguin Books.

7. STUDY OF RELIGIONS
AND SOCIOLOGY

1. INTRODUCTION

Sociology is the study of human societies and the relationships within and between them. A social group may be a family, a religious community, a village or a nation. There are overlaps in both focus and methods between social anthropology (see Part II Chapter 6) and social psychology (see Part II Chapter 8).

Advances in science and technology in the eighteenth and nineteenth centuries encouraged people to believe that there could be a rational explanation for everything and that science could solve all human problems. Auguste Comte (1798–1857 CE), who gave the name to sociology, confidently expected that it would provide the highest level of scientific explanation in establishing the laws of human society itself. It would replace theology in providing an understanding of social hierarchy and moral order. Religion would then disappear.

Classical sociology in the nineteenth century was mainly European. It expanded considerably in the USA in the mid twentieth century. Here the methods of empirical research developed. During the 1960s it became a major social science subject at universities and is currently a popular A level subject in UK schools.

The principles of modern sociology may be summarised as follows.

- Human society involves people entering into relationships with each other. These relationships take many forms and may be described as cultural, economic, political or religious.
- Patterns of human relationships become institutionalised in the course of their reproduction over time and may therefore be referred to as 'social institutions'.

- Institutions may incorporate global influences but local influences remain important.

- In order to participate in societies human beings maintain an understanding of their relationships with others and of the institutions in which they participate, whatever the scale.

- The task for sociologists, therefore, is to capture this understanding in a systematic way and provide explanations of human behaviour which are understandable in terms of everyday life.

Sociology embraces the whole range of human activity from the upbringing of children to gender roles to communities and burial customs, for example, and this makes it a very wide field of study.

2. SOCIOLOGY OF RELIGION

People may often wonder, 'Who am I?' The sociologist would say that personal identity is shaped by society. It is developed in living and communicating with other humans, influenced by the structures and social institutions of society, family, friendship and community. There may also be religion, work and other forms of social organisation, all contributing to the identity of the developing person (see Part II Chapter 9).

All societies incorporate belief systems. In the nineteenth century, with further developments in science and technology, rational and scientific explanations seemed to be taking over from spiritual or mystical ones and religion became less evident and significant in national and individual lives, a process called *secularisation*. However, the major religions of the world continue to flourish and survive, even in the face of industrialisation and materialism. Events in the twentieth and twenty-first centuries, such as wars, terrorism and environmental damage, have contributed to an undermining of confidence in science and technologies alone and have led to a search for alternative beliefs. Such changes in individual and corporate belief systems are areas of particular interest to sociologists of religion.

Religious beliefs also inform the individual what action is good and desirable, and what is bad and to be avoided. Therefore an entire range of values, norms and attitudes derive from religious belief. Sociologists are interested in how certain social organisations like religions use this information to establish power structures to uphold what they believe to be right.

To summarise: religion can be seen as one form of social construction. Sociologists of religion are interested in this particular field of study because, despite *secularisation*, religion remains important to many people in their daily lives, giving meaning and value to their experiences. Religions create social groupings and communities of interest for sociologists.

In order to study religions, sociologists, like the rest of us, have, throughout the history of the discipline, sought to define what they mean by 'religions'. Historically they have worked with two types of definition.

The first is substantive, and seeks to define what religion is, whilst the second is functional and concentrates on what religion does.

3. DEVELOPMENT OF IDEAS

There is an important overlap between the development of sociology and the work of anthropologists (see Part II Chapter 6). The study of early anthropologists was based on the evolutionary theory that religion progressed alongside material advancement, from *primitive* to developed. These anthropologists, like many later sociologists, could be said to have as their focus the functional aspects of religion.

Emile Durkheim, (1858–1917 CE) in *The Elementary Forms of the Religious Life* (1912, translated and published in English in 1915), proposed that rituals perform vital social functions. These functions include the generation of social solidarity, sustaining society, particularly in times of trouble and difficulty, and providing a moral order of shared values. He thought that as changes occur and society becomes more fragmented, the firm moral base provided by religion would lessen and there would be more crime and higher suicide rates.

Durkheim studied the coming together of communities for religious purposes to worship and celebrate their community/shared identity. Some sociologists suggest that, in functional terms, a contemporary equivalent is the coming together of communities to celebrate their shared values and beliefs, for example through 'worshipping' a football team. The function or effect of such activity is the same as the effect of traditional religion, that is, it reinforces social bonds and shared values.

Durkheim also provided one of the most commonly used definitions of religion:

> A unified system of beliefs and practices relative to sacred things, that is to say things set apart and forbidden – beliefs and practices which unite into one moral unity called a church, all those who adhere to them. (1915: 47)

Karl Marx (1818–83 CE) also considered religion to be something created by humans – that is, a social product. The primary functions of religion, Marx claimed, were to generate order in society and to legitimate injustice in the relationship between workers and capitalists. Thus, those in power used the idea of a divinely ordained social order to keep the workers or proletariat subjugated. Furthermore, the idea of heaven and the rewards of life after death were used to make the proletariat accept their poverty and lack of status and power. Religion, for Marx, was a tool to maintain the status quo between the few 'haves' and the many 'have nots'. This explains why Marx famously defined religion as

> The sigh of the oppressed creature, the heart of a heartless world, just as it is the spirit of a spiritless situation. It is the opium of the people.

> (Cited in Hall and Scott, 2001: 24)

Some later Marxists have revised Marx's theory on religion and used it as a tool for achieving equality. The liberation theologians of Latin America criticise both the State and the Church for legitimating social arrangements of great oppression and exploitation. Liberation theologians use Marxist analysis of power relations in society and the teaching of Christianity to criticise social inequality and work against injustice. For these later Marxists religion is a generator of social change.

Max Weber (1864–1920 CE), who, with Durkheim, is one of the founding fathers of sociology of religion, also believed that religion was an important source of ideas and practices that shaped the social world. He believed that religion can be a source of both social change and social order. Weber's main contention was that with the rationalisation of modern social and economic organisation the significance of religion will fade.

Weber's great work on the sociology of religion, entitled *The Protestant Ethic and the Spirit of Capitalism* (1904–5; translated and published in English in 1930), was the first major study of the interaction of religion and social organisation. Weber suggests that there exists a relationship between economic activity and religious belief which enables the individual to express their sense of divine calling in their daily work. He suggests that ideas of hard work and frugality in *Protestantism* and capitalism mutually reinforce one another as worldly economic success can be seen as a sign of being one of God's chosen ones.

One of Weber's strengths was his work on religions other than Christianity and Judaism. He wrote a sociology of Hinduism and Buddhism called *The Religion of India* (translated and published in English in 1958). Weber was also the first sociologist to propose and explain how the industrialised world would become more secular – a theory developed by the sociologist Bryan Wilson (d. 2004) and known as *secularisation*. Weber stated that religious explanations of events in the world, such as miracles, would gradually be taken over by scientific explanations – a process he called 'rationalisation'.

4. SECULARISATION – OR NOT?

Social theorists such as Weber and, later, Wilson posit a decline in religion as *secularisation* becomes more dominant due to increasing technological advances and the move from rural to urban living which characterises much of modern life. Others argue that modernisation simply gives opportunity for the rise of new forms of religion, perhaps more individual, mystical and private spiritualities.

Two significant areas of growth in religious expression are New Religious Movements and New Age spiritualities. Both forms of religion have expanded considerably in the industrial world in the twentieth and twenty-first centuries. Both also have expanded as people have been more able to make individual choices about their religious preferences. However, sociologist Steve Bruce argues that numerically these religions are small and the effects on the lives of believers, especially for the New Age, are not significant in the way traditional religions have been.

One intriguing characteristic to consider is the extent to which these movements draw inspiration from Hindu and Buddhist religious ideas and practices. Does this indicate a dissatisfaction or disillusionment with the current technological, urban, materialistic society? Is it helped by higher levels of education and the global spread of ideas? Or is it that in a society which values individualism it simply gives people more choice?

In some parts of the world there is a major resurgence of religion, for example Christianity in sub-Saharan Africa, or Islam in the Middle East. It is still the case that most sociological studies are carried out in Europe and the USA. A question we need to think about is how relevant these methods and ideas are to forms of religion in Asian, African or Far Eastern countries where the development and cultural significance of religion is quite considerably different from post-Enlightenment Europe. Here the sacred and the secular may not be appropriate categories or they may be much less clearly defined and religion may be characterised by informal structures and organisation with permeable boundaries such as those between Shinto and Buddhism in Japan.

5. METHODS USED

A key concern of all social sciences is to assemble empirical data from which to work. This data is generated by means of both historical investigation and contemporary social research. There are two key types of data collected by sociologists and psychologists (see Part II Chapter 8):

- Quantitative – Quantitative research relies on large-scale surveys of religious belief, ethical values and churchgoing practices. Data is collected from questionnaires, church attendance and other statistics, public records and Gallup polls. Such data may be used in conjunction with other data such as political involvement or moral values to establish the links between them and the influence of religion in people's lives. Statistical analysis is an important element of quantitative studies.

- Qualitative – The qualitative approach to the social investigation of religion relies on small-scale studies of communities or groups and uses participant observation and in-depth interviews in a similar way to the other disciplines, such as phenomenology and anthropology (see Chapters 4 and 6). Data thus collected helps to construct descriptions and theories of the social character and significance of particular religious groups.

An example of quantitative research is Robin Gill's examination of records of churchgoing in the nineteenth and twentieth centuries. He found that the amount of decline in church attendance had been exaggerated and was more to do with over-enthusiastic building by the Victorian Church of England and the provision of Free Churches than lack of faith. So, the fact that many are now used as warehouses, arts centres or Hindu temples is not necessarily evidence of secularisation.

Grace Davie has surveyed data of church attendance which reveals the emergence of a distinctive religious style in Britain and elsewhere, to which she gives the phrase 'believing without belonging'. She discovered that while only 9 per cent of the population regularly attends a public act of worship, between 50 per cent and 60 per cent claim to believe in God, to have had religious or transcendent experience, to pray regularly and to watch religious programmes on television. She argues that this demonstrates that religion has not been abandoned, but it has become more privatised. It must be pointed out that other sociologists may draw alternative conclusions from the same data.

Qualitative research often involves participant observation where the researcher takes part in religious events and is able to speak with participants to gain a deeper understanding of the social setting. For example, sociologists such as Eileen Barker have investigated some of the New Religious Movements which have proliferated in the last hundred years, seeking to identify the causes for their popularity by studying individuals and making small case studies of specific groups.

Many sociological studies of religion include both quantitative and qualitative methods in order to arrive at balanced and rich descriptions of beliefs and practices. Sociologists aim to bring objectivity and impartiality to their reflections as they consider the data collected – which is what they mean by their study having a scientific approach.

Increasingly there is a recognition of the role of religion in post-modern societies in both the developed and the developing worlds. The way religion operates within society and its potential for influencing future change remains an absorbing field of study for sociology of religion.

BIBLIOGRAPHY

Barker, Eileen (1989), *New Religious Movements: A Practical Introduction*, London: HMSO.

Bruce, Steve (1985), *Religion in Modern Britain*, Oxford: Oxford University Press.

Davie, Grace (1994), *Religion in Britain Since 1945: Believing Without Belonging*, Oxford: Blackwell.

Gill, Robin (1993), *The Myth of the Empty Church*, London: SPCK.

Gill, Robin (2003), *The 'Empty' Church Revisited*, Aldershot: Ashgate.

Durkheim, Emile [1912] (1995), *The Elementary Forms of the Religious Life*, tr. Karen Fields, New York: Free Press.

Martin, David (2005), *On Secularization: Towards a Revised General Theory*, Aldershot: Ashgate.

Northcott, Michael S. (1999), 'Sociological Approaches' in P. Connolly (ed.) *Approaches to the Study of Religion*, London: Cassell, 193–225.

Scott, Julie F. and Irene Hall (2001), 'Religion and Sociology' in I. Markham and T. Ruparell (eds) *Encountering Religion*, Oxford: Blackwell, 21–43.

Weber, Max [1904] (1958), *The Protestant Ethic and The Spirit of Capitalism*, tr. Talcott Parsons, London: Allen and Unwin.

8. STUDY OF RELIGIONS AND PSYCHOLOGY

1. INTRODUCTION

The Greek words 'psyche' (soul, mind or spirit) and 'logos' (word, science or knowledge) are the roots of the word 'psychology'. It might be said that all religions are interested in knowledge of the soul and whether the soul exists. However, the term 'psychology' as it is generally used in English applies to the scientific study of the mind.

Psychology of religion is not a mainstream part of traditional psychology courses at universities. Though some important psychologists, such as Michael Argyle, have had much to say on religion, the subject of religion is not of central importance in the academic discipline of psychology. Nevertheless, you may find specific modules on psychology of religion in some psychology departments, but you are more likely to find such modules in Religious Studies departments. Many students choose successfully to combine undergraduate studies in religion and psychology.

2. PSYCHOLOGY AND RELIGION

Psychology is a young subject and the link between psychology and religion is comparatively recent. In the 1840s Ludwig Feuerbach (1804–72 CE) asserted that religious beliefs were no more than a projection of human desires and hopes onto a fictitious being we call 'God'. Human beings are, for Feuerbach, no more than their material nature and other ideas are a product of the imagination.

Psychology of religion has often been an outsider mode of understanding religion with categories and concepts that are secular and alien to the subject of religion. The psychoanalyst Sigmund Freud (1856–1939 CE), for example, defined all religion as 'wish fulfilment' and 'universal obsessional neurosis'. In *Totem and Taboo* (1913) and *The Future of an Illusion* (1927) Freud related religion to infantile desires and declared the truths of religions to be illusory. Freud's claim that religion arises out of human psychology is a reductive position. In this type of psychology of religion, *outsiders* define the reasons for, and meaning of, religion.

The *reductive* approach to psychology of religion has led to many interesting pieces of research, for the question arises: if religions are not the product of some kind of God or transcendent cause, why do people believe in them? Furthermore, are there any psychological benefits or dangers for believers in religion?

The most influential early scholar to link psychology and religion was William James (1842–1910 CE). James' *Varieties of Religious Experience* (1902) was based on his Edinburgh Gifford series of lectures in which he offered psychological and philosophical perspectives on religious experiences. James' approach compared different kinds of religious experience from different religious traditions, focusing particularly on conversion and mystical experiences, and seeing mysticism as at the heart of religions. James' interest in religious experience has been continued in both philosophy and psychology.

A number of psychologists have examined the relationship between religion and mental health, which was also an interest of William James. For example, Kate Loewenthal and M. Cinnerella have compared the efficacy of religion, medication and psychotherapy in dealing with depression and schizophrenia. Other psychologists have carried out studies of the effects of prayer and the role of religious ritual in coping with stress.

Another important area in psychology of religion relates to faith development. The psychologists Piaget and Erikson developed 'stage-theories' in the growth and development of humans in the 1960s. They suggested that as people move from infanthood to childhood, to adolescence and adulthood they go through different stages of cognitive development. These ideas were used by Kohlberg in his examination of moral development among individuals and further explored by Fowler in his studies on levels of religious faith.

A useful way of differentiating the many approaches of psychology is to define the main types of psychological investigation. But we must recognise that there are hundreds of schools within these fields.

- Psychology as a rigorous scientific discipline with sub-fields in, for example, experimental psychology, clinical psychology, social psychology, educational psychology and psychotherapy.

- Psychotherapy as a sub-discipline of psychology with four further divisions into: cognitive psychotherapy, behavioural psychotherapy, psychoanalytic psychotherapy and humanistic psychotherapy. Of these, only the last, humanistic psychotherapy, is especially concerned with religious psychology.

There is a different kind of relationship between religion and psychology as a discipline of study than religion and some of the other academic approaches covered in this book. In the area of religious psychology there is an overlap in the interests of both religious believers and psychologists studying religious beliefs. The following sections will concentrate on this specific aspect of psychology.

3. RELIGIOUS PSYCHOLOGY

There is a significant difference between 'psychology of religion' and 'religious psychology'. There are many psychologists whose perspective on religion is less reductive than those who assert that religions exist as a result of chemical events in the mind or social psychological needs. Their representations of religion may not be the same as those of specific religious traditions, yet there is a common sympathy of interest in the idea of a spiritual or *numinous* aspect to human existence.

One way of picturing the relationship between psychology and religion is not to consider the interests of psychology in religion but rather the interests of religion in psychology. The psychological perspectives of psychotherapists in particular have added weight to the evidence and beliefs of many religious insiders. In an increasingly secular scientific environment, empirical assertions about human psychology that seem to support religious conceptions have been grasped quickly and tightly. Thus the discovery of the modern Self in psychology has become the keystone of a religious psychology that seeks support for the concept of the Spiritual Self.

Of all the early psychologists Carl Jung (1875–1961 CE) has become a foundation figure for humanistic psychology. This is despite Jung's ambivalence to traditional religion and undoubted wariness regarding religious superstition. Foremost among Jung's ideas commonly used in religious psychology are:

- The 'collective unconscious' – Jung hypothesised beyond Freud's conception of a personal unconscious that affects our conscious choices and preoccupations, especially through dreams, to a universal or collective unconscious. Jung considered the similarity of content and themes across cultural traditions to be evidence of this collective unconscious.

- Archetypes – The universal content of dreams, Jung argued, has specific aspects, which may be found across geography, history and in different religious traditions and cultures. These aspects have recognisable features which define them as 'archetypes', and may occur in religious myths and in dreams. Examples of archetypes are the notion of the Hero, the Mother, the Wise Woman and the Trickster. Jungian archetypes are frequently used to explain the meaning of systems that involve types of personality such as astrology and Tarot.

- Synchronicity – One significant difference between religious worldviews and secular worldviews is in the definition of meaningful events. The secular worldview tends to define meaning in terms of chance and probability, while the religious worldview prioritises fate and destiny. The former emphasises causal and mundane explanations while the latter emphasises acausal and spiritual explanations. Jung stated that synchronistic events were those which had acausal properties. For example, synchronicity is used to explain the unlikely concurrence of events or perceptions, such as the intuition of a distant friend's or relative's death which is then discovered to be true. Synchronicity seems to support a perspective on the world as spiritually meaningful.

- Individuation – Jung's conception of the pathway to achieve 'wholeness' and recover individual well-being against the fractures to personality caused by human development was termed 'individuation'. For Jung the best means to achieve this end was through psychotherapy. Religions have many ways of achieving wholeness, from mental disciplines such as meditation for Buddhists to the mental and physical postures of Hindu yoga to living a life of self-sacrifice and humility such as is practised by Christian Franciscans.

4. HUMANISTIC AND TRANSPERSONAL PSYCHOLOGIES

Although it was Jung who coined the term 'transpersonal' in relation to psychotherapy, the religious psychology that has developed with this label is far removed from his original concept. Some of the techniques for achieving individuation are similar to Jung's form of psychotherapy but many of the concepts have changed.

One key part of transpersonal psychology is the idea of Human Potential (an idea coined by the writer Aldous Huxley). Human Potential grew out of two themes developing in psychotherapy. The first theme was being developed by psychologists interested in a holistic approach to psychotherapy – these included Rollo May, Virginia Satir, Carl Rogers and Fritz Perls. Their interests were not only in psychotherapy as an aid to recovery from pathology, or mental illness, but also in developmental psychotherapy for 'ordinary' healthy individuals. The principles, and some practices, behind these therapies differed in detail but each derives from a holistic concept of the individual with potential to develop in areas of creativity and relationship.

The second theme that influenced Human Potential evolved from a more *spiritual* interest of transpersonal psychotherapy. This area of humanistic psychology focused on three aspects of the human psyche and its potentialities:

- Psychological events related primarily to spiritual experiences

- The evidence these experiences offered for a religious reality underpinning the mundane world

- The means of achieving these experiences

The key originators of psychotherapeutic understandings of such religious experiences included Abraham Maslow (1908–70 CE). Maslow had been researching experiences of clarity and understanding that may be called 'moments of enlightenment', equivalent to James Joyce's term 'epiphany' or the Japanese Zen Buddhist concept of *satori* – which Maslow later called 'peak experiences'. He posited a 'hierarchy of needs' whereby after achieving 'basic order needs' of food, shelter and clothing humans require 'higher order needs', which include attaining status and recognition, and the need to express creative abilities and talents. These higher order expressions could lead to the clarity of self-knowledge and understanding gained in 'peak experiences'. Maslow further developed the theory that people who had achieved the ability to find such levels of clarity were 'self-actualised'.

5. PSYCHOTECHNOLOGIES AND THE SEARCH FOR THE HIGHER SELF

Transpersonal psychotherapy has designated itself a wider role than traditional psychologies, that is as formative and of value for 'normal neurotics' rather than a crisis response to those with mental illness. As an instrumental spiritual practice and technique Marilyn Ferguson has called this mode of psychotherapy 'psychotechnology'.

Of the multiplicity of psychotechnologies available there are two key areas of practice worth examining here: relationships and past lives.

Relationships – The central theme of humanistic and transpersonal psychotherapy is relationships. M. Scott Peck, a psychologist whose focus was in relationship therapy, has been enormously influential in this area with the book *The Road Less Travelled* (1978). His emphasis on a psychology that is informed by religious beliefs and integration of a concept of 'spiritual growth' is reminiscent of Jung's idea of individuation and Maslow's idea of self-actualisation.

Past Lives – The use of hypnosis and the practice of regression therapy in traditional psychology is accepted scientific methodology to uncover repressed memories. A number of psychotechnologies take the phenomena of repressed memory and regression further to memories of former lives. Of the many past-life psychotherapists one of the most influential is Roger Woolger. Woolger's *Other Lives, Other Selves* (1990) is an examination of those whose memories include events from other historical individuals' lives. Woolger's conclusion is that these are accurate memories of past lives, and therefore evidence for reincarnation.

Connected to past-life therapy are the mass of writings on Out-of-Body Experiences (OBEs) and Near-Death Experiences (NDEs). The former provide evidence for religious insiders of a soul that exists apart from the body and the latter that this soul migrates to other realms. It is only a short conceptual step to conceive that the soul migrates to other bodies and that investigation and recovery of memories from these past selves comes within the ambit of psychotherapeutic practice.

BIBLIOGRAPHY

Beit-Hallami, Benjamin and Michael Argyle (1997), *The Psychology of Religious Behaviour, Belief and Experience*, London: Routledge.

Connolly, Peter (1999), 'Psychological Approaches' in P. Connolly (ed.) *Approaches to the Study of Religion*, London: Cassell, 135–92.

Fox, Mark (2003), *Religion, Spirituality and Near Death Experiences*, London: Routledge.

Fowler, James (1995), *Stages of Faith: The Psychology of Human Development and the Quest for Meaning*, London: Harper and Row.

Freud, Sigmund (1927, Standard Edition 1962, reprinted 1991), *The Future of an Illusion*, London: Penguin Freud Library Vol. 12: 183–241.

James, William (1902, reprint 1982, centenary edition 2002), *The Varieties of Religious Experience: A Study in Human Nature*, London: Penguin Books.

Jung, Carl (1933, reprint 1995), *Modern Man in Search of a Soul*, London: Routledge.

Loewenthal, Kate (2000), *The Psychology of Religion: A Short Introduction*, London: Oneworld.

Peck, M. Scott (1978), *The Road Less Travelled: A New Psychology of Love, Traditional Values and Spiritual Growth*, New York: Simon and Schuster.

Woolger, Roger (1990), *Other Lives, Other Selves*, London, Aquarian.

9. STUDY OF RELIGIONS AND IDENTITY

1. INTRODUCTION

> 'Identity' has increasingly become a *key category* for human self-understanding, nowhere more so than in looking at the role of religions in the world.

> Eric Lott, 2005: 11

There is no individual university subject or field that encompasses the topic of identity. Yet it could be argued that questions about identity lie at the heart of the search for knowledge in many subjects studied at universities. When we ask the question 'Who am I?' we begin a process of discovery that includes understanding ourselves, others and the world around us. Identity is a key feature of anthropology, psychology, sociology, philosophy and study of religions. Issues about identity are central to the human quest for meaning, or as the author Douglas Adams, the author of *The Hitchhiker's Guide to the Galaxy*, defines this quest, 'life, the Universe and everything'.

So, to what does the word 'identity' refer? The author and scholar Madan Sarup suggests that the notion of identity is 'the story we tell of ourselves . . . which is also the story others tell of us' (1996: 3). Each story is in some way unique to the individual, and so there are as many identities as there are individuals. This aspect can be termed 'personal identity'. But it is also true that these stories are written in specific historical, social and cultural contexts which construct not only how the story is told but also the main elements of each story. We share important characteristics of our stories with others.

This aspect can be termed 'social identity'. So questions about identity relate to what these unique (personal) and shared (social) characteristics might be.

> Religion has long been regarded by social scientists and psychologists as a key source of identity formation and maintenance, ranging from personal conversion experiences to collective association with fellow believers.
>
> Coleman and Collins, 2004: 3

Those religions that define an everlasting soul or self suggest that the soul is the central shared characteristic of identity. Some forms of Hinduism, for example, state that the soul (*atman*) is identical to the essence of every other living being and also with the Ultimate Reality (*Brahman*). Identity in this sense means 'the same as'. Therefore both personal and social identities for these Hindus are the same at a spiritual level. Hindus also have a group identity which distinguishes them from Buddhists or Christians, for example. This may be marked out by diet, ways of greeting one another and dress. However, there is always much more to this issue of identity than theological or philosophical statements about how we are in essence everlasting and unchanging. This is because identity is also about differentiations between people and it is equally a process that involves change.

Given the very wide range of discourses that discuss identity we can only provide the briefest snapshot of some key areas where the notion of identity has had a significant impact on the study of religions in this section. You will see in each of the sub-sections on 'Gender and Identity in Religions', 'National and Ethnic Identities in Religions' and 'Spiritual Identities' a mixture of the themes relating to the meaning of identity discussed above: that is, personal and social identities; essential and differentiated identities; unchanging and changing identities.

2. GENDER AND IDENTITY IN RELIGIONS

The first thing to note is that the idea of gender difference is not the same as the idea of sex difference. Sex differences are about the biological and physiological differences between men and women. Gender differences, on the other hand, are about the historical, social, cultural and religious perceptions of how women and men are different and how they should act in the world.

The scholar of religions Ursula King has defined two ways that religion and gender are entwined: first she highlights the fact that 'religions are an important source for the understanding of gender'. That is to say, in the books, beliefs and practices of different religions scholars can discover descriptions and definitions of the ways that women and men should behave and what roles they should have in society, according to each religion. There have, for example, been long debates about the ability and rights of women to take on priestly roles in the Church of England. Until the ordination of women was agreed in 1987 many theologians argued that such a role was not appropriate for Christian women.

The second way religions and gender are related, King states, is that 'religious beliefs and practices are themselves significantly shaped by gender perspectives' (1997: 647). Until the end of the nineteenth century arguments against women's ability to carry out any of the training required for Christian priesthood were supported by spurious biological arguments that women were innately less intelligent and less able. This gender perspective of many earlier societies was enshrined in laws that denied women a vote and access to universities. So, religion and wider cultural perspectives on gender influence each other.

The *feminist* critique and reappraisal of religions suggests that identity as it has been constructed by traditional religions and wider society is the product of *patriarchy*. The patriarchal construction of identity is one where the male is normative and holds the power. Women are denied positions of authority within the organisational structures of many traditional religions and therefore often have only a peripheral role in the history of the religion. Equally, the language used for God in some religions is predominantly male. The consequences of patriarchal systems of thought in religions for female identity are many. Women come to be seen, in Simone de Beauvoir's words, as 'the second sex'. Without power and authority and, in most religions until the twentieth century, education, women have been seen as 'the other'. Women have therefore been forced into a collective and social identity of silence with only a few instances (in relation to men) of female personal identity which provide examples of committed religious leadership.

Feminist scholars of religion suggest that patriarchal history has covered over the stories of those powerful women that existed in the histories of religions. Therefore scholars such as Rita Gross seek to uncover patriarchal his-stories and recover some of the her-stories that exist in the historical record. Gross has worked predominantly on the history of Buddhism, but the same process is part of work in other religions too. These women can provide significant role models with which contemporary women can identify. Another helpful enterprise for greater gender balance in religions is the recovery of the feminine aspects of Ultimate Reality, whether it is the feminine form of the terms for Spirit in Christianity, the *Goddesses* of Hinduism or the feminine principle in the Sikh vision of the Transcendent.

A further gender critique offered by scholars of religion is that many other scholars, both historical and contemporary, write their books without recognising the existence and significance of women in religions. This is often unconscious, a product of the patriarchal presumption of the importance of men's activities in religion. This position is called 'sexism of omission' or oversight. Such oversight is still present in studies of identity in religion where even the important contribution by Hans Mol, *Identity and the Sacred: A Sketch for a New Social Scientific Theory of Religion* (1976), has no mention of gender as a key category for this new theory. Current scholars of religion emphasise the need to consider both women's and men's roles in the history of religions. And on a very practical level we encourage students to use gender-inclusive language in their essays and not always use the pronouns 'he' or 'him' to refer to all people, both male and female (see Part II Chapter 13).

3. NATIONAL AND ETHNIC IDENTITIES IN RELIGIONS

Religious identity is closely tied to ethnic and national identity. Even the names we sometimes use for religions are no more than labels that identify a specific culture or place – for example, Hindu is a reference to 'people from the Indus' (many 'Hindus' refer to their religious beliefs as *sanatana dharma*, which means 'eternal teaching'). In part this is because religion has been an integral part of the history and social institutions of peoples and nations. However, in the European Christian world there has, since the eighteenth-century *Enlightenment*, been an increasing division between the state and religion. It might be argued that British, Danish or French social identities are no longer significantly shaped by religious beliefs. But for those who are religious, both personal and social identities are mixed with ingredients that include their ethnic and national identities.

In our plural world, religious, ethnic and national identities are ever more complex. Scholars of religion have written on this in their investigations into *diaspora* religions. As ethnic groups have migrated to other countries they have taken with them their culture – religious beliefs, language and values. Thus, especially for the naturalised second generation, individuals see their identity as many-layered – from kinship or family relationships to religious tradition to ethnic background and nationality. Eleanor Nesbitt has illustrated this point clearly in her ethnographic studies on young Coventrian Punjabis and Gujaratis (2004). These young people define themselves in different ways for different situations. They may define themselves as British Hindus or British Sikhs in one context, British Asian or Indian in another, according to their *samaj* (society or community) or their specific devotional religious group, such as Ravidasi or Valmiki, in another context. Identity construction, Nesbitt points out, is a process that is ever changing. You might consider how you define your identity. Do you identify yourself in different ways in different contexts?

> An individual constructs and presents any one of a number of possible social identities, depending on the situation. Like a player concealing a deck of cards from the other contestants, the individual pulls out a knave – or a religion, an ethnicity, a lifestyle – as the context deems a particular choice desirable or appropriate.
>
> Robin Cohen (cited in Coleman and Collins, 2004: 6)

Another way of uncovering identity is by using census data. The 2001 UK census provides significant *quantitative* data on the variety of religious beliefs and ethnic groups within the UK population. The variety of religions and ethnicities within the UK support our assertion that there are a great number of personal and social identities. The excellent web site http://www.statistics.gov.uk/census2001 allows you to navigate this data with a specific section on 'Ethnicity and Religion'.

4. SPIRITUAL IDENTITIES

A growing feature of the way individuals label their religious orientation is in terms of spirituality. People will say that they are interested in spirituality but that they are not interested in religious institutions. This new way of defining personal religious identity is linked with the 'New Age' and alternative religions, but it is also a way that those in traditional religions describe their spiritual growth and development. However, for alternative religious seekers claiming a fixed identity limited by any one traditional religion is no longer appropriate for them.

According to the sociologist Steve Bruce, the current interest in spiritualities is part of the process of *secularisation*. He argues that the growth in consumer culture means that people become more customer-oriented towards religion. Instead of staying with a religious tradition people are now choosing from a variety of sources the beliefs and practices that fit with their lifestyles (see Bruce, *Religion in Modern Britain* 1994). This has been called the 'pick 'n' mix' approach to religions. So, for Steve Bruce, New Age spiritualities are a product of consumer capitalism and evidence of the movement away from religion to a secular society. Do you think that the UK is becoming more *secular*? Is spirituality a pick 'n' mix type of consumer religion?

One of the central notions underlying why individuals choose teachings and practices from a variety of sources is the 'perennial philosophy'. This is the idea that at their core religions and spiritual paths are teaching the same central Truths. So, for example, the idea that the world has been created by a spiritual power is a common belief, as is the idea that human life has a purpose and meaning beyond biological and material reasons. This is a perspective that has also been suggested by some of the traditional religions, as, for example, in the saying often quoted from the Hindu *Vedas* that 'the truth is one, the paths to it are many' or 'that which is one, the sages speak of in various terms'.

One key feature of the contemporary religious scene is that instead of inheriting a religious identity individuals choose or even construct one for themselves. People create their spiritual identities in many ways. They often adopt mystical teachings from the major traditional religions. There are many forms of mysticism but, just as with the idea of spirituality, people in alternative spiritualities assert that the mystics express core teachings and a common goal that are true across religions. It is therefore not surprising to see in bookshops translations of the Muslim *Sufi* poet Rumi (1207–73 CE) and the Medieval Christian mystic Meister Eckhart (1260–1327 CE), and descriptions of the Jewish *Kabbalah* alongside one another, or within the same books.

In alternative spiritualities personal identity is defined by selections of teachings and practices followed by each individual. Social identity is less clearly defined. However there are networks and small communities such as Findhorn in Scotland that focus on developing aspects of these spiritual teachings.

There are also more diffuse networks located in places such as Totnes, Glastonbury, Hebden Bridge and Kendal where social identity is formed by significant groups of the population participating in alternative events and using alternative therapies.

BIBLIOGRAPHY

Beattie, Tina and Ursula King (eds) (2004), *Gender, Religion and Diversity: Cross-Cultural Perspectives*, London: Continuum.

Bruce, Steve (1985), *Religion in Modern Britain*, Oxford: Oxford University Press.

Coleman, Simon and Peter Collins (eds) (2004), *Religion, Identity and Change: Perspectives on Global Transformations*, Aldershot: Ashgate.

Gross, Rita (1993), *Buddhism After Patriarchy: A Feminist History Analysis, and Reconstruction of Buddhism*, Albany: State University of New York Press.

Heelas, Paul, Linda Woodhead, Benjamin Seel, Bronislaw Szerszynski and Karen Tusting (2004), *The Spiritual Revolution: Why Religion is Giving Way to Spirituality*, Oxford: Blackwell.

King, Ursula (1993, 2nd ed.), *Women and Spirituality: Voices of Protest and Promise*, London: Macmillan.

Lott, Eric (2005), *Religious Faith, Human Identity*, Bangalore: Asian Trading Corporation and United Theological College.

Mernissi, Fatima (1993), *The Forgotten Queens of Islam*, London: Polity.

Mol, Hans (1976), *Identity and the Sacred: A Sketch for a New Social-Scientific Theory of Religion*, Oxford: Blackwell.

Nesbitt, Eleanor (2004), '"I'm a Gujarati Lohari and a Vaishnav as Well": Religious Identity Formation among Young Coventrian Punjabis and Gujaratis' in Coleman, Simon and Peter Collins (eds) *Religion, Identity and Change: Perspectives on Global Transformations*, Aldershot: Ashgate, 174–90.

Sarup, Madan (1996), *Identity, Culture and the Postmodern World*, Edinburgh: Edinburgh University Press.

Singh, Nicky-Guninder Kaur (1993), *The Feminine Principle in the Sikh Vision of the Transcendent*, Cambridge: Cambridge University Press.

PART III
Study Skills in Religious Studies

10. GETTING STARTED

1. INTRODUCTION

You cannot settle down to study effectively unless you know what you are doing and why you are doing it. At all levels – what you are doing with your life, what you are doing at university, what you are doing in a Religious Studies class – the more informed and aware you are, the better will be your motivation and your ability to study. This introduction aims to take some of the worry out of daily life and to help you be focused on the tasks at hand. Do not be surprised to find, among the information on study skills, a number of hints on what might be described as life skills. During the time you are at university, the two are inextricably linked.

2. WHY GO TO UNIVERSITY?

You may be a seeker after knowledge and/or you may hope for a better career with a degree and/or you may be going for the social life and/or you may be going because it is expected of you. Whatever your reasons, graduation day comes and you have to find a job. People expect a university degree to improve career prospects, but have you ever wondered why? Unless you become a teacher, Religious Studies may not become the main focus of your employment, though we have indicated its usefulness in many professions (see Part I Introduction). But employers are mainly looking for transferable skills and you have to make sure your prospective employer knows that you have them.

2.1 General transferable skills

In general, university graduates are self-motivating.

- They are good at time-management.

- They can work under pressure.

- They can meet deadlines.

- They have learned from their seminars how to be team-players and how to work as part of a group.

- They have shown that they are well-rounded individuals by taking an active part in at least one of the sporting, social or intellectual activities offered by university societies or clubs.

Other skills you will develop as a Religious Studies undergraduate include the ability to:

- communicate ideas and arguments clearly and by a variety of oral and visual means

- use primary data and sources

- work collaboratively

- undertake independent study and research

- use IT for data capture and to support research and presentations

- show critical awareness of personal beliefs, commitments and prejudices

- demonstrate the skills of communication of ideas including at dissertation length

- relate presentation of ideas, principles and theories to an intended audience

- reflect and interact with ideas and arguments of others

- work collaboratively in ways which maximise individual talents

- have sophisticated time management and skills of self-directed study

- show independence of thought

2.2 A special word to mature or non-standard entry students

Some mature students often worry too much. If you are a mature student coming to university for the first time, you may have many problems to contend with that students straight from school do not have. You may have family commitments, perhaps even young children and all the worries about child-care that parenthood entails. Your university may provide good quality, low-cost child care. This is worth finding out about. You may have got out of the habit of studying, writing essays and sitting exams and the young students may seem incredibly self-confident and knowledgeable. You will soon get back into the way of studying and you would not have been admitted to university if you did not have the ability to succeed, so there is no reason to compare your talents unfavourably with those of younger students. For some reason, many mature students feel that they have to do better than the younger students to prove to themselves that they can do as well. If this sounds like you, calm down. Your maturity gives you extra skills, particularly in time management and communication. It is always a joy to teach mature students because of their high level of motivation and the fact that they have a great deal of life experience to draw on, which is particularly important for a subject like Religious Studies, and because they ask lots of questions. Also, just because their lives are more complex, they are usually exceptionally well organised. If any domestic crises should occur, or if you are having difficulty with any aspect of study, you will find that members of staff are very understanding and supportive.

3. WHY CHOOSE RELIGIOUS STUDIES?

Some of us study religions for their own sake, as a window on life and on what motivates people in different cultures. Others have religious commitments and want to further knowledge of their own and different religious traditions. Others do it because it complements other courses, anthropology, psychology, theology, philosophy or history, for example. The best reason for doing Religious Studies is because you like it, but it also brings its own bonus of transferable skills, a bonus which often goes unrecognised and which will be of lifelong service to you.

3.1 Religious Studies transferable skills

When you reach the giddy heights of final year and start looking around for a career, you might like to point out to a prospective employer how your study of religion, whether you did it at Honours level or whether you did it only for a year, has made you the very person for the job.

These are some of the Religious Studies transferable skills you can expect to develop as a student, taken from the national benchmark statements for Theology and Religious Studies (TRS):

The qualities of mind that a competent student should acquire by studying TRS may be characterised as follows:

- The ability to understand how people have thought and acted in contexts other than the student's own, how beliefs, doctrines and practices have developed within particular social and cultural contexts and how religious traditions have changed over time. (A degree of 'cultural shock' may be involved in study of the past, as well as in the encounter with the beliefs, doctrines and practices of contemporary others.)

- The ability to read and use texts both critically and empathetically, while addressing such questions as genre, content, context, perspective, purpose, original and potential meaning, and the effect of translation if the text is not read in the original language.

- The appreciation of the complexity of different mentalities, social behaviours and aesthetic responses, and of the ways they have been shaped by beliefs and values, and conversely how beliefs, sacred texts and art forms have been shaped by society and politics.

- Sensitivity to the problems of religious language and experience, and to the issues of multiple and conflicting interpretations of language and symbols, texts and traditions. Simplistic, literalising or doctrinaire explanations are less likely to be advanced by a student of TRS.

- Appreciation of both the interconnectedness of and internal tensions within a system of beliefs and practices.

- Basic critical and analytical skills: a recognition that statements should be tested, that evidence and arguments are subject to assessment, that the interpreter's role demands critical evaluation.

- The ability to employ a variety of methods of study in analysing material, to think independently, set tasks and solve problems.

- The capacity to give a clear and accurate account of a subject, marshal arguments in a mature way and engage in debate and dialogue with respect for the opposite case or different viewpoint.

Such qualities of mind may be regarded as intellectual skills and competencies arising from study of the subject. As in other academic disciplines, they are undergirded by commitment to integrity in pursuit of understanding and to being true to the object(s) of study, and by recognition of the contested and provisional nature of knowledge and understanding.

Perhaps the greatest advantage that Religious Studies brings is the enhancement to your thinking skills. Few subjects bring together the many different ways of thinking that Religious Studies demands. You need to think clearly, methodically, logically and creatively. You will be able to seek out and evaluate evidence. You also will have developed skills in empathetic and sympathetic understanding – being able to 'walk in another's shoes'. You will also have creativity and flair. Not only will you have bright ideas but, additionally, you will be able to analyse them and explain how they work.

4.   BE IN THE KNOW ABOUT YOUR SUBJECT

4.1.   The course handbook

Most courses have a course handbook with essential information such as course content, reading lists, a timetable, what the assessment procedures are, whether or not you have to register for exams and if so, where and when. The course book may also tell you how essays and other written work should be presented. Always read the course book carefully, and refer to it from time to time, just to remind yourself of what you should be doing at any given point in the term.

4.2   The noticeboard

Find out where the subject noticeboard is and keep a regular eye on it. Any changes to class times and locations will be posted there, sometimes at short notice. It is the place to look for tutorial lists, exam details, extra lectures and seminars and so on.

4.3   The departmental administrator

The departmental or faculty office may not be open to student enquiries all day. Find out when the administrator is available.

This is where to go if you miss a lecture and need the handout, if you want to double-check dates and places for exams, if you can't get hold of a particular lecturer, if you change your address and so on.

4.4 Computing support

Even if you are a complete technophobe, you must find out how to make the most of the available computing facilities. Increasingly, university departments insist that written work be done on a word processor. Some even ask for work to be submitted in an electronic form so that it may be scanned for plagiarism.

On a more positive note, a word processor makes editing and revising your work very much easier; you have the benefit of a spellchecker, and you produce an attractive final copy, which will put the marker in a good mood. For larger pieces of work, such as dissertations and theses, the word processor may provide an appropriate layout.

There will almost certainly be courses on computing for new students and they are well worth attending, whether you are computer literate or a complete beginner. You will save a lot of time and effort if you find out how much your computer can do for you. The infinitely patient computing-support personnel are equally good at helping nervous beginners and more adventurous, technically minded users.

The computer is also essential for gathering information from library catalogues and from the Internet. There are a variety of excellent search engines to find information on religions as well as subject gateways such as Academic Information Religion Subject Index (http://www.academicinfo. net/religindex.html) and Virtual Religion Index (http://virtual-religion.net/vri). Equally, a number of universities provide portals for secure information on religions. Increasingly, religious groups use the web to share information and some groups exist only in a virtual sense with services and ceremonies conducted on the World Wide Web.

You will probably be given an e-mail address in your first week. Check your e-mail frequently because this is how your tutors, lecturers or the departmental administrator will get in touch if they need to contact you urgently, and it will be appreciated by your tutor if you send an e-mail if you have to miss a class and s/he may be able to let you have missed handouts.

Before you even apply to a university, explore the web sites of universities you might consider going to. They might help you decide which university to choose.

5.   WHERE TO STUDY

If you are lucky enough to have a separate study, your own desk or dining-room table, then there are few problems. It is possible to work from an armchair, or even a bed, though you will need proper back support and some kind of book rest or portable table on which to write. Most people find working for a period of time is easier at a table or desk. Posture is very important. Some people are able to read on buses and trains, though trying to write in a swaying carriage can be very difficult. Some main-line trains, however, now have computer points.

Lighting is also important. Avoid having a light source immediately behind you, or a strong light which reflects glare from white paper. An angled lamp is ideal if you can get one.

Don't forget that the room you are working in should be well ventilated, and heated in winter! Too low or too high a temperature or working in a stuffy room can make concentration difficult.

It is not easy to study if there's noise from the hi-fi or TV in the next room. It is sometimes difficult for other people to appreciate how hard you need to concentrate when you are studying. So that you can think with the intensity required to make sense of new areas of study it is best that you ensure that the people around you understand your study plans and know when to leave you alone.

6.   STUDY MATERIALS

These can take many forms. There are your text books and
the course materials, and there may in some modules be
audio-visual materials like cassettes and videos. Many courses
now include teaching materials available on the World Wide
Web or on intranets specifically for university users.

Remember that these are not the only sources you can draw
on. Novels, newspapers, magazines, photographs, local
sources (scrapbooks, diaries and people themselves!), television, radio discussion programmes and films can also provide
much useful material. It will all depend on the kind of work
you are doing. Observation is the key. Look out for religious
festivals and public or community religious events – participation at these events helps you understand the lived reality
of living religions. Visit holy sites and shrines when on holiday
or travelling. *Religions in the UK: Directory 2001–03* can
give you details of where these are.

You will soon begin to accumulate quite large amounts of
these materials. It is therefore important to begin to be systematic about the way you store the material at an early stage
in your studying. You can develop your own system of labelled
cards, folders and boxes. Being a successful student depends as
much upon being able to access material quickly when you
need it as upon remembering the details of the material itself.

7.   A NOTE ON MANAGING YOURSELF

- Take responsibility for your learning

- Accurately assess your strengths and weaknesses

- Ask for help when you need it – at the beginning of the
  process rather than at the end

- Cultivate your sense of humour

- Do something pleasurable after a study session or the com-
  pletion of a major assignment

- Avoid 'crash' study sessions or last-minute assignment writing. It follows that you should avoid fatigue and when possible use relaxation techniques to enhance study time

- Maintain a 'space' of your own for your work

- Maintain organised files. Loose-leaf (binder) notebooks are useful for note taking since they allow additional material to be inserted as need arises

- Set priorities. Decide what subject or task needs immediate attention

- Maintain continuity of study so that work does not pile up

- Break large tasks/assignments/readings into manageable subtasks, and schedule each subtask

- Set reasonable standards and goals for your efforts

8.   GETTING ORGANISED

In their book entitled *How to Be Organized in Spite of Yourself* (1999), based on the premise that 'no organizational system will work for everyone', Roberta Roesch and Sunny Schlenger provide ten different systems to match the ten 'standard' student personality types. The book also includes quizzes designed to tell you which 'type' you are.

Here are the types, with brief descriptions:

- The Perfectionist Plus – Accustomed to doing well in school. Cannot begin an assignment because s/he cannot bear the thought of falling below the 'ideal' mark or standard of performance that s/he has set for herself.

- The Hopper – Easily distracted – by television, children, boy/girlfriend, mealtime, other books (unrelated to assignment topic), the sounds of nature, or the desire to be 'doing something else'. Wavers between the assignment and any excuse to close a book.

- Allergic to Detail – Finds that research gets in the way of a desire to express her/his own thoughts. Enjoys generalisation and sweeping – often unsupported or inadequately reasoned – conclusions that convey her/his personal opinion. In theological and religious studies, the assignments of the Allergic often read like sermons or editorials.

- The Fence Sitter – A competent researcher who cannot make up her/his mind about how to approach a question or project. Closely related to:

- The Cliff Hanger – May begin as a Fence Sitter. But soon the question becomes: 'Will I have the assignment ready by Tuesday noon? After all, it's already 11.30.'

- Everything Out – An energetic sort, who decides to put her/his life on hold while s/he devotes day and night to the Topic. The antitype of the Hopper, the EO will forego sex, food and religious feasts to improve the mark on the next assignment. [Not to be confused with the Perfectionist.]

- Nothing Out – Having read St Augustine, the NO feels predestined to receive a mark not higher than 50 on the assignment, or decides s/he does not like the topic or that the tutor is an idiot (etc.). Invests minimal effort and discovers s/he was right about the mark all along.

- Right Angler – The operant questions for the Angler are neither 'What am I being asked to do?', nor 'How can I best answer the questions asked', but 'Where is my tutor coming from?' and 'What sort of response would s/he most like to have?' An amateur psychologist.

- The Pack Rat – An expert hunter-gatherer of detail. Unfortunately, discovers that s/he cannot accommodate 30,000 words of expert opinion in a 1,500-word assignment.

- The Total Slob – Some of us are. Most of us can improve.

BIBLIOGRAPHY

Roesch, Roberta and Sunny Schlenger (1999), *How to Be Organized in Spite of Yourself*, New York: Signet.

Weller, Paul (ed.) [1997] (3rd ed. 2003), *Religions in the UK: Directory 2001–03*, Derby: Multi-Faith Centre at the University of Derby in association with the Inter-Faith Network for the United Kingdom.

11. LEARNING, READING
AND ASSESSMENT

1. LECTURES

First-year Religious Studies classes can be quite large. A certain amount of noise is inevitable, particularly during the winter term when everybody seems to have coughs and colds. Coughs, inexplicably, get worse during lectures. Therefore, it is a good idea to arrive in good time and get a seat quite near the front where there is less chance of being distracted and you will be able to hear. If the lecturer is inaudible or if the visual aids are not visible, let the lecturer know at once. If you have a hearing problem consult the university's special needs advisor. If you have a motor or visual problem and cannot take notes, ask the lecturer if you can use a tape-recorder. Tape-recorders should not be used by anyone without permission.

Lecturing styles vary quite a lot and so you must be able to adapt your note-taking and listening. Most lecturers provide a course outline in the course handbook and it is a good idea to take a look at this and get a general picture of where the lecturers are heading. Some lecturers follow a published book (sometimes their own). If there is no suitable book to refer to, you may well get a handout at the lecture or handouts may be collected in a course handbook. If there is such a course handbook make sure you take it with you. If the lecturer sticks closely to the handout, it might be enough just to make marginal notes on it. If there is no handout, or if the handout is extra to the content of the lecture, be sure to take notes. You may think you will remember it all but you won't. A good lecturer will have planned the lecture and it will have a structure. In fact, even though the lecturer may sound quite spontaneous, the lecture should have been constructed in sections and paragraphs like a well-thought-out essay. The lecturer may tell you the plan at the start of the lecture. Try to structure your notes accordingly. Use bullet points and numbers where possible. Use a different coloured pen to highlight key terms and VIPs (Very Important Points). This will help with exam revision. You would be very exceptional if your concentration did not lapse occasionally in lectures but train yourself to wake up rapidly if the lecturer gives any VIP signals.

Not all lecturers are charismatic and riveting. You may have to make a big effort to stop your attention from wandering. On these occasions, you could try active rather than passive listening. Imagine you are in a radio discussion programme and will have to respond to what the lecturer is saying. What can you agree with? What would you question? What stimulates you to think in fresh directions? Not only will this game help to keep you awake but it will also help you to take good notes.

1.1 Before the lecture

As you start to think about getting ready to go to a lecture, on your way to the lecture and while waiting for the lecture to begin, prepare by asking yourself some questions:

- Do I know the title of the lecture?

- What is it?

- What could be the subject of the lecture?

- How might the subject of this lecture relate to others in the series?

- How does it relate to the previous lecture?

- Will it develop any of the points from the previous lecture(s)?

- How might the subject relate to other course components?

- Are there any points of connection?

- Or is the subject unique to this particular area of study?

- What do I already know about this subject?

- What do I want to know about this subject?

- Have any of my studies or other lectures covered this subject, or any part of it?

- What interests me about this subject?

- What issues do I think are important?

- What do I want to get from this lecture?

- Given what I know about the lecturer, what can I expect to learn from the lecture?

In other words, you will get more out of a lecture

- if you prepare for it beforehand

- if you arrive at the lecture room having thought about the subject

- if you have expectations or questions that you hope will be fulfilled and answered

- above all, if you have done all prescribed reading listed in the syllabus or indicative bibliography as preparation.

1.2 During the lecture

Going to a lecture is not a passive exercise – a matter of turning up and simply listening to what is being said. The problem with 'just listening' is that whilst most of us think we are listening, we are only actually hearing – the words go in one ear, and out the other.

During the course of the lecture, you need to take a positive and active role in what is going on. As opposed to just sitting and listening while the lecturer is speaking, try to imagine that you are having a conversation with him or her. Ask yourself:

1. What is actually being said?
   Is it right?

What is being implied? Do I agree?
Are there any other possible implications?

2. Is this consistent with other ideas/concepts/pieces of information already mentioned in the lecture?
How do the various pieces fit in with or relate to each other?
Is there a pattern or structure emerging?

3. Where is this line of thought going?
Why is it going in this direction?
Where could it go?
If I was lecturing, in which direction would I develop it?

4. Is there an overall shape or structure to this lecture?
If so, what are the key ideas? concepts? arguments?
What supporting ideas, concepts or sub-arguments are being built upon this structure? Does it work?

5. Is the lecturer answering any of the questions I want answered?
Is he or she addressing any of the issues that interest or concern me?
What am I expected to do with this information?
How can I use it?

By being more positive, and by taking a more active role in listening to what is being said, you will get much more out of the lecture.

1.3 Lecture signposts

It is usually fair to say that most of the lecturers you will come across will make this task easy for you by using verbal signposts. At a simple level, this may amount to nothing more than being given an outline of what is going to be said at the start of the lecture. But on another level, lecturers often use verbal phrases to indicate what is going on in the lecture. So during the course of the lecture, look out for key/important/significant phrases:

- Firstly, secondly, thirdly …; the main points of the argument are 1, 1A, 1B, 1C, 2, 2A …; the argument breaks down like this …

- Further … Even further … What is more …

- On the one hand … On the other hand …

- An illustration of this … An example of this …

- Now, what this shows … Now, what this proves … (conclusion)

- Thus … Therefore … So to conclude …

- One implication of this … This might entail … What might follow from this …

- Now what does this really mean? …

These are signposts and 'linking phrases' – they hold the argument and the structure of the lecture together. You need to be able to identify them.

1.4   Lecture notes

Taking notes during a lecture is a difficult business and requires you to have a high degree of concentration. It is one of the most important skills that you will need to develop.

As a lecturer may speak for fifty minutes to an hour and a half, it is all too easy to fall into the trap of thinking that you have to get every word and every syllable spoken onto paper. Unless you have taken a course in shorthand, this will be physically impossible!

Even if it were possible, you wouldn't actually learn anything from the lecture – you would be too busy scribbling away to have time to think about and digest the significance of what is being said. What is important is to take notes selectively:

- Don't expect to make a perfect replica of the lecturer's notes; that must never be your aim.

- Some lecturers speak very quickly, with the result that you will always find yourself being left behind, concentrating more on what has been said than on what is being said, and so will miss something important.

- Concentrate on and aim to get the bare essentials. To get the bare essentials, listen for the verbal signposts and linking phrases.

Sometimes this is easy, but you will need to concentrate, particularly when you are dealing with sub-points or sub-arguments.

- Try to get down the shape and structure of the lecture; the shape and structure of the argument; the sequence of ideas/arguments/concepts.

- Do not write incomprehensible notes – they will be of no use to you.

- Write down only phrases/key words – not whole sentences. Keep notes legible.

- Do not be afraid to check whether you can interrupt the lecturer; if you don't understand something, or you are not sure of something that was said, either stop the lecturer or, if they are not happy about that, bring it up at the end.

- Ask him or her to expand/explain/provide an example. It is crucial that you don't get lost or left behind. Make sure you understand what is being said.

At the end of a lecture, there will probably be a short time for questions. Do not be afraid to ask. If, however, you cannot bring yourself to speak in front of a large audience, have a private word with the lecturer afterwards. Questions are useful feedback for lecturers, who need to know whether their lectures are pitched at the right level.

Always read through, and make sense of, your lecture notes the same night, while the lecture is still fresh in your mind, and if there is recommended reading to do, do it as soon as possible after the lecture. You might like to revise your lecture notes with a friend, in the hope that your absent moments do not coincide and that, if one of you has a gap in your notes, the other can supply the deficiency. By the same token, if you miss a lecture, borrow notes for the same lecture from at least two people.

Make a special effort to get to the last lecture of every lecture block or module. This is when you might pick up hints about exam questions.

2. TUTORIALS

Tutorials are probably the most efficient and enjoyable way of learning. They usually consist of one, two or a small group of students and a tutor. Right from the beginning, get to know at least some of the people in your tutorial group. It can be a great help to go for coffee after a tutorial and talk about Religious Studies with people who are at the same stage as you. It means that you will have people you know to sit next to in lectures. It also means that, if for any reason you have to miss a lecture, you can borrow lecture notes easily.

The official aims of a tutorial are to consider an essay that you have written, to reinforce lectures, to clarify any points in the lectures that you did not understand and to explore topics in more depth than can be attempted in lectures, perhaps moving on to related topics that were not covered in the lecture but which are still relevant to the course. To get the most out of a tutorial, you need to tell your tutor where your difficulties and interests lie and be able to discuss your written work in some depth.

Do not be afraid of asking something that seems very basic or even silly or giving a wrong answer. In tutorials, you are very unlikely to be assessed on what you know (although you should clarify any criteria for assessment with your tutor). If tutors award a mark for tutorial performance at all (and not all courses have tutorial assessment) it will be based on attendance and participation. If you make a mistake in a tutorial, you and your tutor can get to the bottom of it and clear up any misunderstandings. Better to make a mistake orally than in written exams or essays.

Attendance at tutorials is usually compulsory and if your attendance is poor, the tutor will be obliged to inform the course organiser and your director of studies or personal tutor. This is partly for academic reasons, to make sure you are not falling behind with your work. It is also for pastoral reasons, to make sure you are not ill or in some kind of difficulty. Please try to let your tutor know if you are going to be absent. Believe it or not, your tutor will worry about you. Because tutors are the members of university staff with whom students come into contact most frequently, they are often the first person that a student will consult about a non-academic problem.

Discussion plays a large part in tutorials. Each tutor has his or her own style of teaching, but you may well find that you spend a lot of time in your first year practising language skills, such as learning how to pronounce key terms in the different languages used in different religions. Your problem-solving skills will undoubtedly be extended. You will also look at texts and apply your growing knowledge of religious concepts, under your tutor's guidance, to all the varieties of written material associated with religious traditions.

Your tutor may well give you some clues about essay writing. If your tutor spends part of a tutorial giving a taught lesson rather than a discussion or practical session, look for structure. Can you spot possible section headings for an essay? For example, your tutor may divide a tutorial on the religious *diaspora* of Hinduism into different parts on Hindus in India, West Africa, the UK and Canada. Make each of these into a section, add a short introductory paragraph and a short closing paragraph and you have a well constructed essay on the Hindu religious *diaspora*. If you are stuck with your essay, seek help from your tutor. Do not expect any help that would give you an unfair advantage, but your tutor may be able to discuss the topic with you in a very general way and sometimes the very act of explaining your difficulty to someone who understands can help you to solve your problem yourself.

In the last tutorial before the exams, keep your ears tuned in for clues. Your tutor may be authorised to tell you a bit about the exam layout. You may go over old papers in the tutorial and be given hints on question spotting or hints on structuring answers. If the course has changed recently, past papers can put you in a complete panic by asking about things you have not covered, and your tutor will be able to reassure you. If the tutor does some exam revision with you, which topics are the focus of attention? After the exam, be sure to ask your tutor about any mistakes you have made if you cannot see for yourself how to put them right.

The better prepared you are for a tutorial, the more you will get out of it. Obviously, you will do any reading that the tutor has asked you to do and you should attempt any essays and written exercises that you are given as homework. It is not unusual for students to find some exercises very difficult at first. If that happens, do as much as you can and try to work out exactly where you are finding difficulties. Let your tutor see your attempt, however pathetic it looks to you. Do not be embarrassed; you are not going to be the only one in the group who has a problem. The tutor needs to know what areas of the course need extra consolidation and which bits are easy enough for you to revise on your own. If there is no set preparation, make sure that you have understood the lectures and the recommended reading that goes with them. Tell the tutor about the bits that are not clear.

If you have any special needs, tell your tutors if there is anything they can do to help. For example, if you are partially deaf and need to lip read, suggest to the tutor that you sit where you can see the tutor's face clearly, in good lighting, and ask the tutor to help by speaking clearly. If the tutor lapses and starts talking to the blackboard, a quick reminder will not cause any offence and would actually be appreciated by the tutor.

3. SEMINARS

Between the full-scale large lecture and the small, intimate tutorial lies the seminar. It is a rather vague term because different teachers approach seminars in different ways. Some treat them as large tutorials and others treat them as small lectures. There should be more opportunity for questions and comments in a seminar, so come well prepared in order to contribute but, because it is a larger gathering, you must also let other people speak and take care not to monopolise the teacher's time. Do not expect the same level of individual attention that you get in tutorials.

Seminars are not just a supplement to lectures, but an important way of learning and thinking. Unlike lectures, seminars are two-way, not one-way; learning takes place through conversations, questions and answers, differences of opinions. In other words, seminars are a responsive and interactive way of learning. You learn by interacting with, and responding to, the views of others in the group. Some of the styles may be called workshops in different contexts.

Seminars can take a number of different forms:

- working and discussing set material in pairs/threes/fours

- discussing a topic with the tutor and other students present on a subject which has been prepared beforehand by everyone equally

- one of the group makes a presentation in turn which is then discussed

- completing a task in small groups, and reporting back to the rest of the group

- role-playing and empathy exercises

- watching videos/listening to tapes – resources learning

Seminars, therefore, provide varied means of getting to grips with a subject and enable you to develop a range of different skills.

But perhaps the biggest obstacle to benefiting from seminar discussions is the strange belief that you cannot learn anything from other students – that you can only learn from respected 'authorities', ie, the tutor. And so the question usually arises: why bother with seminars? There are a number of reasons why you should bother with seminars. They provide:

- relief from the one-way monologue of a lecture; they allow you to talk back, question, argue and explore ideas that you find exciting and significant

- relief from studying on your own; they allow you to try to put into words the various viewpoints and ideas uncovered during your reading, to test and experiment with your own opinions and arguments, to hear what others in a group say in response

- an opportunity to explore issues raised by lecture and seminar material, to articulate problems or points which seem particularly relevant or exciting for you, to help others in their thinking about such issues

- a chance to share and try out your ideas with other people

- a chance to hear and respond to other people's ideas

- a way of sharing problems and discovering that you are not the only one experiencing these difficulties

- a way of developing your communication skills and power of expression

As you can see, there are a great number of benefits to be gained from seminars. But, as with lectures, it is important that you actively prepare beforehand for a seminar if you are to get maximum benefit.

Seminars are not just a matter of turning up and listening to what is being said –they are not something that simply 'happens'; you need to be ready, you need to be prepared for a seminar. That way you will know what to expect, and what is expected. So, as with lectures, ask yourself a number of questions:

- think about the subject you are going to discuss

- ask yourself what you already know about this subject

- ask yourself about the directions you would like the seminar to go and the ideas you want to explore

- read the work that has been set for the seminar

- ask yourself what the central ideas are, what their significance is, and what the implications of these ideas might be

- try to arrive with a list of key questions/issues that you want to bring up and explore

- ask yourself whether you have any evidence/experiences that you think are relevant and significant and want to share

- ask yourself how this subject relates to other subject areas

- ask yourself what the points of connection are

- ask yourself where the main areas of disagreement are

- think about what you want to get from the seminar; have an aim/goal in mind, for example, to have certain ideas clarified or certain areas explored

- come prepared with two/three points to make

It is vital that you do not feel intimidated, shy or frightened of speaking. Seminars are successful only if you are willing to contribute, and you have as much right to put forward an opinion or viewpoint as anyone else.

Remember: you only get out of a seminar what you are willing to put in.

3.1 Strategies for seminars

There is no recipe for a good seminar. The following guidelines are designed to indicate modes, or strategies, for participation. You will be able to decide for yourself which strategy to employ on which occasion(s):

- Ask questions. Ask them of your fellow students, of the tutor and about the material. Asking questions is a respectable way of moving a discussion along.

- Read 'around' the subject. In addition to required material, locate a 'dissenting' view and present it for seminar consideration.

- Rehearse what you want to say before you say it. Feeling comfortable in discussion does not mean that you should blurt out everything that pops into your head. A good discussion depends on listening carefully to what is being said, then formulating a response or reaction to it. Speak when the opportunity presents itself, and when you are satisfied with your response.

- Formulate short questions and responses beforehand.

4. ORAL PRESENTATIONS

Some tutors expect students to give oral presentations in tutorials and/or seminars. It is not very likely that this will happen at the start of the first year. By the time you have to give a talk, you will be familiar with your subject and friendly with the other members of the tutorial group, who are all going to have to go through the same torment.

Your oral presentation will be based on a written paper, produced with all the skills you would use for writing an essay. Some tutors will be quite content if you simply read from your written paper. Your fellow students, on the other hand, may find this boring. So:

- Try to keep your voice interested and interesting.

- Be sufficiently well prepared so that your nose is not always buried in your paper.

- Mark the important points in your paper (probably topic sentences) with a highlighter pen, so that you can find your way at a glance.

- As you speak, watch your fellow students and make eye contact with them and the tutor.

- Smile.

- Invite questions and comments and be prepared to deal with them.

- Do not be afraid to admit that you do not have all the answers.

- With your tutor's permission, make use of any appropriate audio-visual aids (whiteboard, overhead projector, computer screen, audio and video recordings).

- Provide a handout if you think it would be useful.

- Flag possible issues for discussion in case discussion is slow at the beginning.

5. READING

Your lecturers will recommend reading to be done along with the lecture course. You will get the most out of the lectures and the reading if they keep pace with each other. Sometimes, a lecture course will follow a set text book quite closely but there will almost certainly be additional reading so that you can broaden your knowledge of the subject and assess different points of view.

Your first task is to get hold of the book or article. There will be some texts that are recommended for purchase and knowing that students are always short of money, lecturers will keep this list to a minimum. Watch the noticeboards or search web sites for second-hand copies. If you are tempted to buy an old edition, check with your tutor that there have not been too many changes. Books that you do not have to buy will be in the library. Make sure that you are first in the queue – there are always more students than books. Right from the start, get to know your library and how it works. Familiarise yourself with the shelf numbers where Religious Studies books are kept, and enjoy browsing among them. Practise using the online catalogue. It will tell you not only where to find books, but also whether they have been borrowed and when they are due back. If a book that you need has been borrowed, you may be able to recall it. Just ask at the service desk. There may be more that one place to find books. For example, there are the ordinary open shelves that make up most of the library but, in addition, especially when books are recommended for essays and there is likely to be a huge demand for them, books may be put in a special section of the library where they are on very short loans, say three hours at a time. There are also usually separate sections for reference books such as the *Dictionary of Christian Ethics* or encyclopaedias of religion. If you have problems, the most valuable resource in a library is the librarian. Ask a member of the library staff for help.

The best academic writers, particularly those who are directing their writing towards first-year students, try very hard to keep their writing clear and easy to read. However, it is not always possible to express very complex ideas in very simple language. Furthermore, learning a new subject means learning all the terminology of that subject. Occasionally, some of the reading that you do will seem very dry and difficult. Persist. Gradually, you will build up your reading muscles to Olympic standards. This is yet another of the benefits of a university education; no act of parliament, company report or small print on a contract will daunt you after graduation.

The first two parts of this book will have given you some indication of the type of reading you will have to do. From it you can see that some topics are more readable than others, but none of it is exactly easy. It demands what is called 'active reading'. You really have to work and think along with the text. For this reason, do not underestimate how long a chapter will take and do not set yourself too big a chunk of reading in one sitting. Apart from the introductory chapter of each book, you are unlikely to be able to read a chapter straight through from beginning to end. Take a bit at a time. If there are exercises in the book you are reading, do the exercises for each section as you go along. If there are no exercises, set yourself some. Take notes. Try to rephrase the text in your own words as you do so. Occasionally, joint study sessions with other members of your tutorial group might be helpful. Together, you might make more sense of difficult passages, think of some good examples or be able to test each other.

The moment you sit down with a book, make sure you note down all the necessary bibliographical detail including page numbers. Be sure to mark exact quotations in your notes. If you find something you may wish to quote word for word, make sure that you get every detail right, including the punctuation. If it contains what looks like an error or is gender insensitive, put [sic] after the error and then everyone will know that you are quoting accurately and the mistake is not yours. Much of your note-taking will consist of paraphrases or summaries of the text but often a passage from a book will spark off your own ideas. Make a note of the passage and write down your responses to the passage at once, or you will almost certainly forget what they were. Be sure that you make it very clear which notes are exact quotes, which are paraphrases and which are your own thoughts. (Use different colours of pen.) It is very easy, at a later date, to think an idea is your own when, in fact, you have found it in the course of your reading. Strangely, it is even possible to have an original idea and then to convince yourself that you read it somewhere.

Notes are an aid to learning, not a substitute for it. You should not just copy down words for future reference. Try to take notes in your own words. Before you can do that, you have to understand what you have read and that is the first step in learning. The physical act of writing something down will help to fix it in your mind. Also, you have to be selective and, in being selective, you begin to exercise your critical judgement. If you then take notes of your notes, you repeat these learning steps. If you are using your own book or a photocopy, you will probably use a highlighter pen. Do not be tempted to use a highlighter or underlining as a way of not having to read something that you suspect is important but is too hard to understand. Make the effort then and there. If it is important enough to highlight, it is important enough to learn. Do not highlight indiscriminately or you will not be able to see the wood for the trees.

Only once you have done the recommended reading should you start looking for additional reading. The set books might make recommendations, or you could browse along the library shelves, or you could do a search on the library online catalogue. Subject searches are not always reliable. Sometimes keywords in the title can produce better results. This might produce such a wealth of material that you don't know where to start. A good guide is the number of times a book or article is cited in other people's bibliographies. You will see from this which texts are important reading. If you need help, ask your tutor.

When you are browsing, use the contents page or abstract to identify useful and interesting bits and scan read to find the bits you want. Do not start at the beginning and try to work your way through. First make sure that the book or article has something to offer.

5.1 Four types of reading

Broadly speaking, there are four different ways of reading, and consequently four different aims associated with each kind. These are:

Type	Aim	Purpose
Skimming	for main ideas	to discern and assess
Receptive	listening to the author	to analyse and comprehend
Reflective	responding to the author	to evaluate and apply for yourself
Scanning	for special points	to locate an area for study

You should try to make your reading as 'active' as possible, rather than trying to soak up everything that is being said. Think about what you are reading.

Ask yourself:

- Do I agree with this? Why?

- Do I disagree with this? Why?

- How does this fit in with other books I have read?

- How might this fit in with the argument I am developing?

Rather than merely copying out relevant pieces of text, try to re-express what you have read in your own words, as concisely as possible. Try not to copy out more than two or three sentences of the author's own words; you will then avoid becoming reliant on the text, and the style in which it is written and you will avoid the danger of plagiarism.

The author may make the task of reading easier for you by either breaking up the argument into sections or sub-sections, or by using various signposts. Your reading will be much more structured if you try to identify these guides. Try to look for:

The hierarchy of ideas	– level one:	main argument
	– level two:	chapters
	– level three:	sections
	– level four:	paragraphs
Signals	– *italics*	
	– <u>underlining</u>	
	– CAPITALS	
	– **bold text**	
	– boxed items	
	– 1, 2 … numbered items	

Above all, try to read critically – in other words, make a note of questions that occur to you as you read. This is helpful because it motivates you and gives you a purpose in your reading – it focuses and directs your reading, and forces you to think about the information being presented.

For example, as you read, ask yourself:

- What facts are being presented?

- Does the author contradict him/herself?

- Are the facts complete? Are they up to date?

- Are they plausible and supported by evidence?

- Are some of the facts the author's opinion?

- What exactly are the conclusions?

- Do the conclusions follow from what is said?

- Would other conclusions have been possible?

- How do the conclusions compare with other texts?

- What are the weaknesses of this argument?

- What are the strengths of this argument?

- What implications might follow?

- What is relevant for my topic?

If you persist with questioning what you are reading, you will soon develop a critical attitude.

5.2   A short strategy for reading

1. Survey the table of contents and topical index (if any).

2. Process each heading or section-title in relation to the assigned topic or project.
   i. Is the book 'as a whole' relevant or significant?
   ii. What chapters are worth pursuing?

3. Once you have 'selected' the book and decided which reading strategy (see section 4.1) to use, jot down questions about the content presented.

4. At the end of your reading make a few notes. Correlate these with your questions.

5. Enhance your study of the book by consulting other relevant sources.

For example, a study of the origins of the Cult of the Virgin could be enhanced by looking at slides of famous paintings, or by visiting a church. The material on paintings will probably be in the art or large-book section of the library.

5.3   Using Reference Books and Journals

There are many advantages of using reference books:

• they give you a good introduction to a subject

• they are always available in the library

• they usually have good bibliographic information

Get to know the major general works of reference, such as the *Oxford English Dictionary* and the *Encyclopaedia Britannica*.

Types of reference works for Theology and Religious Studies:

1. Dictionaries and encyclopaedias cover topics such as ethics; theology; particular faiths such as Buddhism; issues, for

example religion and war; religions in general; philosophy and statistics

2. Journals focused on areas such as contemporary religions, ethics or philosophy of religion

The advantages of using journals are:

- they enable you to gain a range of views on a subject
- they give you access to current thinking and ideas on a subject
- journals are always available in the library
- they contain up-to-date book reviews

To make the most efficient use of journals, use indexes and abstracts:

1. Indexes cover a wide subject area and give you enough information to find the article.

2. Abstracts are more subject-specific and give you a summary of each article.

Some indexes and abstracts:

British Humanities Index

Religious and Theological Abstracts

Science of Religion Abstracts

Remember that some journals, reference works such as the multi-volume *Encyclopedia of Religion* in its second edition, indexes and newspapers exist in electronic form. These sources, as well as specialist theological and religious web sites, can provide important information for the course.

If you want to photocopy anything, you must obey the regulations on copyright displayed beside university photocopying machines.

6. EVALUATING WEB SITES

The importance of the web as a research tool and as a resource for information on religions has grown considerably in the last ten years. However, it is a resource that must be used carefully. Any individual with the strangest opinions can construct what looks like a professional and authoritative web site. As an undergraduate you must learn specific skills of discernment and judgement on the quality and veracity of web information. Fortunately, there are a growing number of books and web-based sources to give you directions on how to evaluate the quality of material found on the Internet. Alison Cooke (2001) has provided some useful guidelines on how to assess the quality of web material which can be applied to religious web sites:

- Identify the purpose of a source – does the source seek to justify specific actions or doctrines, for example does it purport to be a justification for violent jihad?

- Assess the coverage of the source – if the site describes Jewish beliefs, is it only the views of a minority such as the Messianic Jews?

- Assess its authority and reputation – if the web site is on Protestantism in England is it produced by the Church of England or a theological faculty, or by an individual?

- Assess the currency and maintenance of a source – are the views and facts expressed out-of-date, for example about the Catholic–Protestant conflicts in Northern Ireland from before the Good Friday agreement?

- Make a comparison with other sources – for example if there is information unfavourable to a New Religious Movement from an ex-member, how does this compare with material from the movement itself or secondary material produced by university web sites and those created by reputable scholars such as Eileen Barker and the organisation INFORM?

There are also a growing number of very good guides about web-based information on religion. For example Lorne Dawson and Douglas Cowan's edited book *Religion Online: Finding Faith on the Internet* (2004), which describes a variety of web-based religious expressions, and Brenda E. Brasher's *Give Me That Online Religion* (2004), which provides a more ethnographic study of cyber and virtual religious activity. In the UK Gary Bunt has also studied Islamic movements online and provided an overview of religion on the Internet in *World Religions: The Good Web Guide* (2001).

FINALLY, IF YOU NEED HELP, ASK THE LIBRARY STAFF!

BIBLIOGRAPHY

Brasher, Brenda E. (2004), *Give Me That Online Religion*, Piscataway, NJ: Rutgers University Press.

Bunt, Gary (2001), *World Religions: The Good Web Guide*, London: Good Web Guide.

Bunt, Gary (2003), *Islam in the Digital Age: e-jihad, Online Fatwas and Cyber Islamic Environments*, London: Pluto Press.

Cooke, Alison [1999] (2nd ed. 2001), *A Guide to Finding Quality Information on the Internet: Selection and Evaluation Strategies*, London: Library Association Publishing.

Dawson, Lorne and Douglas Cowan (2004), *Religion Online: Finding Faith on the Internet*, London: Routledge.

Jones, Lindsay (ed.) (2nd ed. 2005), *Encyclopedia of Religion*, 15 vols, Gale Virtual Library: Thomson Gale.

12. MAKING THE MOST OF ASSESSMENTS

1. ASSESSMENT

There are two kinds of assessment: formative and summative. The formative assessment counts towards your final mark but it also, even more importantly, provides you with the feedback you need to improve your performance and get the most out of the course. The summative assessment is the final test of what you have learned during the course.

The most usual ways of assessing student performance in Religious Studies are essays and dissertations, exercises and examinations. There may be a small proportion of marks for tutorial participation. Most institutions now use continuous assessment, which means that classwork counts towards the final mark.

Exams and essays usually give a very generous amount of choice. This practice can leave a large part of the course unexamined. Therefore, some course organisers prefer to set assignments which require short answers to questions covering a much greater proportion of the course curriculum. These assignments are not necessarily set under exam conditions but might take the place of a class exam. All the comments in the chapters on Examinations and Writing Skills apply equally well to assignments.

Whatever form your assessed classwork takes, the marks are for your benefit as much as for the examiners' benefit. The course handbook should tell you what the marks really mean in terms of whether you have just passed, or passed well, or passed outstandingly. Look at what the course handbook says rather than by comparing yourself with other students. Some years seem to produce a larger number of good students than other years, but the marking criteria stay the same. Look at the markers' comments, good as well as bad, and try to see what makes a good Theology or Religious Studies answer. If a few of you can get together and go over marked essays, exams or assignments, you will get a better picture of what markers are looking for.

2. SELF-DIRECTED LEARNING

Libraries are usually good places to work, if you can manage to ignore occasional, irritating whisperers. You are less likely to fidget and go off to do other things than you are at home. You are not going to be distracted by flatmates, visits to the fridge or your favourite television programme. If you become used to working in the library, you will spend your time there in breaks between classes, potentially useful time which can easily be frittered away.

If you live with other students, make sure that there are clear rules about not interrupting each other's study time. People who play very loud music at three in the morning before a flatmate's exam are not appreciated. Be considerate about your flatmates' exams and essay deadlines and make sure they do the same for you.

By now you will be aware of the length of time that you can work without a break. You may not work effectively for much more than an hour without a break, though some people concentrate for longer. It helps to vary your tasks. Read and make notes for a bit. Then do some practical exercises or test yourself in some other way before going back to reading again. Remember not to set yourself too much reading at any one time.

Sit down to study with a realistic target in mind. Reward yourself (with a walk, a rest, a shower, a computer game, a chat with friends or a phone call) when you have achieved your goal.

Try to avoid working late at night. If you find that it is becoming a habit, revise your time management. If you do find yourself burning the midnight oil, and all students do from time to time, strong black coffee or other highly caffeinated drinks are not the answer. They may give you a short boost, but they will leave you even more tired and so you have another cup, and another. The result is that when you finally go to bed, you can't sleep and you will probably get a headache as well. Try herbal tea or a few deep breaths at an open window instead. If you have the urge to eat, have an apple, a bowl of raisins or pumpkin seeds nearby rather than chocolate, crisps or sweets.

3.   TIME MANAGEMENT

Time management is one of the transferable skills that employers value in a university graduate.

As you progressed through school, you will gradually have been given more and more responsibility for your own time management but between school and university, there is a great leap. You were expected to get to school at the same time every morning and stay there and work until everybody went home. If you were not at a class, somebody wanted to know where you were. Homework was given in comparatively small regular amounts and woe betide you if it was not done.

At university, you may not have a class every day. You may start at nine in the morning, but you might not start until the afternoon. The strict routine of school disappears. You have to make sure you establish a good new routine. Bad time managers start getting up late, missing classes, working late to try to meet deadlines and end up feeling permanently tired, miserable and inadequate. Time management starts when the alarm clock goes off. You need to establish a daily routine.

You also need to keep an eye on the bigger time-management picture. If you were a course organiser, how would you work out the deadline for handing in essays? You can't set an essay too early in the course because the work has not been covered. You want to hand marked essays back in time for students to learn from them before the exams. All course organisers think this way and so the deadlines for essays for all your subjects have a nasty habit of falling around the same time. It is no excuse to say, 'I had three essays to hand in for today. I haven't finished my Religious Studies one. Please can I have an extension?' The time between the setting of the essay and the deadline is very generous, perhaps as much as five weeks. The time to get started is as soon as possible after the essay topics are given out. Furthermore, being quick off the mark means that you get to the library before all the books on the reading list disappear.

If you have had to get a job in order to pay your way through university, keep your priorities clear. University work comes first. When you start missing classes to go to your temporary paid job, something has gone wrong.

Finally, remember to plan some time for relaxation. If you deliberately leave time for having a bit of fun, then you will not be so tempted to let your relaxation time eat into your working time. Also remember that oxygen (that is, being outdoors) is good for the brain.

4. ASSIGNMENT WRITING

Written work – essays, book reviews, portfolios, learning logs, independent studies, dissertations – forms an important and large part of your learning life. Written work involves particular skills, based on the need for all of us to be able to communicate ideas and information as effectively as possible, and Chapter 13 has further information to help you with this.

As a skill, the ability to communicate effectively with other people depends on how well we can structure our thoughts and express our ideas and views in a concise and persuasive way.

The aim of written assignments is to help you develop this skill by testing your ability to:

- analyse a set question or statement

- develop a structured and coherent line of argument or response

- evaluate the significance of the material in front of you

- clearly explain and express your own position or stance in relation to the subject

Researching and writing assignments is therefore an important part of learning how to communicate your thoughts and ideas as clearly as possible. It also gives you the chance to get to grips with a particular issue. After reading, thinking and talking about an area, you may find yourself with a wide range of ideas and opinions that have no clear shape or structure until you try to write down your own version of it and reach your own conclusions in relation to it.

This, however, is hard to do unless you bear two things in mind right from the start:

1. the audience for whom you are writing

2. what the question is asking you to do

Bearing these two things in mind will help you start to shape and organise your thoughts, and give them some direction, goal and purpose.

4.1   Your audience

It is important to keep your audience in mind, because then you will know at what level to 'pitch' your writing. Some people fall into one of two errors: they either see an assignment as a chance to be very 'scholarly' and use a host of technical terms and obscure jargon, or else they see it as a piece of chatty popular literature. The truth is that you need to aim for something in-between. Your audience will usually have two faces:

- The person who will be reading and assessing your writing. This will usually be the tutor. He or she will want to see evidence that you have understood the central issues of the subject being discussed – that you have identified what they are, and the kinds of responses that can be made to them. This person looks at your writing for signs that you have learnt something. He or she will be looking to see if your thinking has developed in the writing you have done. An assignment which only recounts or restates the views of various 'respected' authorities may be a competent piece of exposition, but it says absolutely nothing about what you think

- The stranger – the person who doesn't know who you are or who doesn't know much about the subject being discussed. The former will usually be the external examiner, the latter might be an employer or someone who is considering whether to admit you to a professional course, either of whom might ask to see a sample of your work. Ask yourself: if a stranger were to read my assignment, would he or she understand what I was talking about? If the answer is 'No', then you need to state quite briefly and clearly what the problem being addressed in the assignment is, and how you intend to tackle it.

4.2 Essays and dissertations

You did not get as far as considering university entrance without having gained some skill in writing, but learning to write well is a lifelong task. During your time at university, you will be expected to polish your formal writing style and adapt to the particular conventions of the subject you are writing about.

At university, you will be assessed primarily on what you write and that is inseparable from how you write, because it does not matter how much you know if you cannot express that knowledge on paper in a way that makes sense to the reader.

Make the most of available technology. Many university departments insist on the use of word processors for essays and you should take advantage of computing courses for new students.

4.3   Why write essays?

The obvious answer is 'to prove that you have learnt something'. That, however, is not the only or the best answer. If you tackle your essays in the right way, you will find that they are, in fact, a very important part of the learning process. It is only when you try to explain things in a totally clear and unambiguous way that you begin to expose little gaps in your understanding. So you have to go off and consolidate your learning. More encouragingly, you may find that, as you arrange your ideas, you make connections that you had not seen before. You are putting what you have learnt to work and gaining confidence in handling your new knowledge. The more effort you put into an essay, the more you will benefit.

Essay writing at university level demands knowledge of the conventions of academic discourse and especially of the way of writing accepted within the academic circle of your particular subject. All academic discourse demands attention to detail, not just in the facts and theories you present but also in the manner of presentation. A consistent level of formality is required and an impersonal style where the writer does not get in the way of the subject. Vocabulary and grammar have to be carefully checked to make sure there is no possibility of misunderstandings. Bibliographies and sources have to be cited. You are handling complicated ideas and having to express them clearly. In short, you are becoming expert in the transferable skills of gathering, selecting, organising and communicating information.

Essay writing is a very important part of the learning process.

4.3.1   First read the question

More good students get bad marks because they have misread the question than for any other reason. There are certain recognisable types: *Discuss . . ., Compare and contrast . . ., Describe . . . Analyse . . .*, etc. Think about it. Make sure you undertake the activity asked for.

Everything you write must be relevant to the question. If you include irrelevancies, they will not gain marks and they will even lose marks by taking up space that should have been used for answering the question. Word limits on essays are based on the assumption that every word is necessary and to the point. Lecturers think very, very hard about the exact wording of questions. If you are in any doubt what an essay question means, do not be afraid to ask whoever set it.

4.3.2 The question

It is vital to bear in mind what the question is asking you to do, because you have to understand what the question requires before you start looking at course notes, books, journals and other sources of information. If you understand what the question wants of you, then you can give your reading and thinking direction and focus. Questions are not plucked out of thin air; they are carefully thought about and structured.

As a general rule of thumb, the structure of the question should give you the structure of the answer. Questions usually include directive verbs that tell you how to respond.

- Account for – give a clear statement of the facts about a particular issue or argument. Explain the reasons for, indicate what the relevant circumstances are.

- Analyse – more than just description; this calls for a detailed, in-depth inspection of the individual parts that make up an issue or an argument. You need to grade these parts in order of importance and significance.

- Assess – this asks you to examine closely and then evaluate the relative importance of the issues under discussion. Weigh up strengths and weaknesses, points for and against. In concluding, you have to state your balanced judgement of the material.

- Comment – this is open-ended and asks you to do a variety of tasks: assess, criticise and consider. You must state your view in relation to the material, and support it with relevant evidence, references and explanations.

- Compare/Contrast – this requires you to put different sets of issues or arguments side by side. Compare asks you to look for similarities and resemblances. Contrast asks you to look for dissimilarities and differences.

- Consider – think about, weigh up, assess.

- Criticise – objectively examine the material and give your balanced opinion about its merits and faults.

- Define – give clear and precise meanings; set limits to the area/issue being discussed and show how it relates to other definitions or areas.

- Discuss – examine carefully; analyse; state and support points for and against an argument or issue. Show strengths and weaknesses. Look at all aspects of the debate or issue. Reach an informed, balanced opinion.

- Evaluate – carefully weigh up or decide on the importance or value of an issue or argument. Test its strengths and limitations; state your own view as well as those of authorities.

- Examine – scrutinise and inspect an issue or argument; pay attention to reasons and explanations offered, the context and circumstances in which they arose, their causes and their implications.

- Explain – this is not asking just for a description. You have to interpret material, clarify the direction and thrust of an argument and give reasons for any important features that arise.

- How far/To what extent – don't be fooled by questions of this sort. You are being asked to assess and evaluate the significance of usually one or two arguments or issues within a specific debate. However, this means that you must also be aware of contradictory points of view and counter-arguments, and to include these in your assessment of the evidence or material.

- In what ways – as a 'rule of thumb', assume that this is asking you to present a number of points, in order of relative importance, and to show the points of relation and differences between them.

- Outline – give a structure or framework within which you can then concentrate on the essential points of the argument.

- Review – critically examine and comment on the important aspects of a debate or stages in an argument.

Choose your question wisely. With experience, you will discover the kind of question you are best at.

5. EXAMINATIONS

5.1 Preparing for examinations

You can revise for some subjects the week before exams and use flair or common sense to fill in the gaps. Theology and Religious Studies is not one of them. It is not an impossibly difficult subject but it involves skills which have to be practised and built up over a period of time. If you keep up with lectures and tutorials and do the exercises that are set, you will find the exams are really not a problem.

The best cure for exam nerves is the knowledge that you have studied to the best of your ability. Remind yourself that you are as well prepared as you will ever be and look forward to showing off your knowledge. The examiners want you to pass and they are actively looking to reward you for displaying relevant knowledge. They are not going to try to catch you out. If nerves do begin to get the better of you, before or during the exam, breathe. Breathe very slowly and deeply, counting to seven (a lucky number) as you breathe in. Then see how slowly you can breathe out. Three breaths like this will have you perfectly calm.

Now read the instructions carefully. You will probably be asked to use a fresh examination book for each answer. Remember to put your name on each book, and whatever else you are asked for, for example the name of the module or your tutor's name.

If there is anything you need to ask the invigilator, just put your hand up. It does occasionally happen that misprints occur on exam papers, in spite of careful proof-reading. If something is missed out from the instructions, or they are not clear, the invigilator will be glad to hear about it and will inform the rest of the class. If you run out of paper, feel unwell, need to go to the toilet or need to borrow a pen, put your hand up and the invigilator will come to you.

Read through the questions and choose the ones you are going to do. Decide on the order in which you are going to do them. Make a note of the time at which you will need to start drawing each question to a conclusion. Make a note of the time at which you stop doing each question, finished or not. Do not be tempted to overrun. Use any time left over to check through your answers, but do not start dithering and changing things that were right in the first place. If in doubt, go with your first instincts.

You can improve your exam technique greatly by planning how much time you are going to spend on each question and sticking to it. You know the duration of the exam and you know the number of questions. Assuming that each question is worth the same number of marks, you simply divide the time equally among the questions. This may sound obvious, but it is amazing how many students make a mess of exams because they don't do it.

As you write an exam answer, you pick up marks very rapidly in the first ten or fifteen minutes of writing. After that, the rate at which you collect marks slows down and eventually you reach a plateau. There may even come a point when you end up exposing your ignorance instead of demonstrating your knowledge and your marks could begin to drop. So, obviously, it is better to start three questions than to finish two and leave one unstarted. Before you start an exam, work out how much time you can have for each question. Remember to allow for the time it takes to put your name on the paper and to fill in the other administrative details, question-reading time, thinking time and essay plan time. For essay-type answers, note the time at which you must start to draw each question to a close. Even if you have not completely finished when your time is up, move ruthlessly on to the next question. You may have time to go back and finish it later. Usually, each answer is written in a separate book, but, if this is not the case, leave a big space, or start a new page between answers so that you can go back and add any necessary finishing touches. If there are questions which are divided into sections, work out how much time you can afford to spend on each section and pace yourself accordingly. If you have practised on past papers, you may find that there are some questions you can do quite quickly. In the actual exam, do the quick ones first and divide up the time you have saved among the remaining questions.

5.2   After the exam

When the exam is over, avoid people who ask, 'What did you write for question two?' It is over, finished, and there is nothing you can do to change it. Do not think about it again until you get the results. When you come out of an exam, you may still have a lot of leftover adrenalin. If you have two exams in one day, you need to come down to earth. Take a brisk walk, have something to eat and focus on the next exam.

When you get your exam back, even if you have done brilliantly, look at the examiner's remarks. If you are disappointed with your performance, do you see where you went wrong?

Marks are most commonly lost because of:

- Not reading the instructions and doing one question too few or one too many

- Not reading the question

- Bad time management

- Irrelevance

- Trying to substitute made-up waffle for fact

- Not giving enough examples

Almost as importantly, do you see where and how you did well? Now you know what the examiners are looking for, make sure you give them more of it next time. If you have any problems, ask your tutor.

13. WRITING WITH CONFIDENCE

1. THE WRITING PROCESS

Writing is not a single big task. It is a lot of little tasks which are dealt with under the following headings:

1.1 Collecting data

1.2 Finding a structure

1.3 Planning an assignment

1.4 Polishing

1.5 Preparing for submission

1.6 Proof-reading

1.1 Collecting data

1.1.1 Sources
Most of the information you need will have been covered in lectures and reinforced in tutorials. A good essay, however, shows signs of additional reading which has obviously been well understood and used appropriately.

Make sure you can use libraries to their best advantage. Find your way around online catalogues, encyclopaedias and directories. For example, the new *Encyclopedia of Religion* (2005) is now available online. If you can't find what you are looking for, or don't even know where to start looking, ask the librarians. They will be happy to tell you what is available. You can surf the net for sources including databases which are available to higher-education institutions within the UK, such as ATLA (American Theological Library Association). A word of warning: especially in the early stages, you can be overwhelmed with sources of information and you may not yet know enough to be selective. This is why your teachers provide recommended reading lists. Use them.

1.1.2 Taking notes for essays

When taking notes, keep the exact wording of the essay title in front of you. Constantly ask yourself, 'How does what I'm reading relate to the title?' Noting down your initial reactions to what you are reading can be a good way of getting into the actual writing of your essay.

Since academic writing demands that you provide proper bibliographies listing all the works you have consulted, including web sites, it is particularly important that you record all the necessary bibliographic details. If you take something off the Internet, make sure you record the web site and the date you accessed it.

Only if you are using your own photocopies are highlighter pens acceptable! Do not mark library books. Remember not to break copyright rules when you are photocopying. The rules should be clearly displayed near the university photocopiers. If in doubt, ask a librarian.

1.2 Finding a structure

Students are usually surprised at how much importance markers attach to the structure of essays. Anybody can regurgitate facts. That is not what essay writing is about. Markers are looking for the ability to put the facts to work. Different subjects place a slightly different emphasis on the way facts are manipulated but, in general, you are expected to construct some kind of argument. In this context, argument does not necessarily mean anything confrontational. It simply means that your essay should have a thread running through it.

Sometimes the wording of an essay title suggests a structure: discuss the effects of sex, age and social class on the attitudes of British Hindus to vegetarianism. This rather suggests a brief

introduction, three main discursive, fact-presenting paragraphs and a brief closing paragraph.

If no obvious structure suggests itself, experiment with different ways of writing an essay plan.

1.3   Planning an assignment

Most people find it very useful to have a detailed plan before
they start writing. The idea behind this is that without having
actually written the assignment, you can have a good overview
of the shape and direction of your argument, and at this stage
still rearrange, add, omit or read more material accordingly.

The plan should help you to keep your argument tight and
to the point. As you write, you may want to depart from your
plan as the details of the argument emerge; your plan, like
your timetable, should aid creativity, not kill it!

Your plan may take a variety of forms:

• key words

• a 'spider diagram'

• prose sentences

• a linear structure

Whichever of these you choose, the plan is important because:

• the argument and direction of the piece begins to take shape

• you can test the argument for strengths and weaknesses

• your research, thoughts and information are present in one
  place

• you have a clear overview of your response to the question

• you can see the structure of the assignment – paragraphs,
  connected ideas

• it makes the process of writing up easier and quicker

Your plan should help to ensure that you confront and answer the question directly, without including waffle, waffle disguised as discussion, and irrelevant material.

Some people use mind maps. Put the core idea down on the middle of a piece of paper and let other ideas branch off. These secondary ideas might generate their own branches. Little clusters start to form. These might each form a section or paragraph of your argument. Do not worry if the same idea crops up in two places but ask yourself if that produces a possible link between sections.

You might prefer a more linear plan, like a flow chart, or you might try grouping related facts, listing pros and cons, identifying major themes and so on. These strategies may uncover such possible orders as: a logical progression as a proof unfolds, a chronological progression moving linearly backwards or forwards in time, a spatial structure, dealing with different geographic or topographic areas, a movement from the general to the particular, perhaps stating a hypothesis and testing it on specific examples, or moving from the particular to the general, constructing a hypothesis from the evidence you have set out.

If no plan emerges, do not despair. Sometimes the act of writing brings the necessary insights. Get started on freewriting. To do this, just write as fast as you can, without stopping to think, without lifting your pen, for at least three minutes. It doesn't matter if you write nonsense. At least you have something on paper to expand, re-order and improve.

If you still cannot see a way of making all the data hang together as a whole discussion instead of a jumble of facts, seek help from your tutor.

1.3.1 The introduction

There is nothing quite like being faced with a blank sheet of paper to induce a cold sweat and a rising sense of panic!

The opening sentences of your introduction are probably the most difficult to write and when faced with an empty piece of A4, most people are too anxious just to get something, anything, down on paper – to get going.

Yet in doing this, they are underestimating the absolutely crucial role of the introduction. There are three things which you must try to do in the introduction:

- identify the question

- show that you understand the question

- state how you are going to answer the question

This should then act as a mini-plan for the rest of the assignment; the structure should flow from your introduction. You have to show that you understand what is being asked of you, and that you have a realistic strategy or 'plan of attack' for dealing with the problem. This creates a 'mind set' which helps the reader to get into the correct gear.

But how do I start? What do I write for a first sentence? You need to bear in mind that the job of an introduction is to:

1. introduce the line of discussion or argument – it prepares the way for the main body of your answer to the question, and should do no more than set the scene.

2. act as a statement of intent – this is important for you because it lays out the line of attack along which the assignment will proceed. It is important for your reader because he/she then knows what to expect, and the order in which to expect it.

In the introduction you are therefore committing yourself to a particular course of action. Once you have done this, do not deviate from it! If you do, the reader might suspect that you do not know where you are going, or why you are going there. The reader will think that you have not planned properly.

What is more important is that the introduction creates an impression. As the saying goes, you don't get a second chance to make a first impression – and we all form an impression of someone when we first meet them. The same goes for written work; the first thing the reader meets is the introduction – so it is important to make a good first impression.

In the introduction you should aim to give the reader at least three things:

Parts of Introduction	Function of Parts
1. An evaluation of the subject	Shows you have [a] understood the subject for discussion and [b] have a good grasp of the necessary relevant information
2. An outline of the argument	States how you will proceed because [a] this is the role of the introduction and [b] proves that you have grasped the question
3. A 'bridge' to the first section of the argument	Allows you to move smoothly from your opening remarks to the start of the argument

Your central points must not go into the introduction; simply try to make it as clear, precise, logical and interesting as possible. This way the reader will get a good first impression of both the writing and the writer.

It takes practice to write well. You might find the following pattern useful as a guide:

- assessment of the subject   two sentences

- outline of the argument   two sentences

- 'bridge' to the first section   two sentences
  of the argument

This should help you to keep tight control over the amount of material that you include in your introduction, and force you to be highly selective and critical of what is relevant and what is waffle.

1.3.2   The main text
If you find the six-sentence guideline for the introduction is useful and works for you, then you can change it to the six-paragraph guideline for the main text or 'body' of the

assignment. This guideline is in no way a rigid rule; it is useful because:

- it limits the length, and so contains the problem
- it makes you work within a defined paragraph structure
- you control the writing – the writing does not run away from you
- paragraphs have a clear purpose; they start and finish when you wish
- it forces you to think concisely and answer efficiently

You may need more than six paragraphs, depending on the length of the set assignment; if so, use them. But remember, so long as you set a clear limit, you will have control and confidence. You will not find yourself reaching a point where you say 'enough', and finish off with a flurry of vague concluding sentences.

1.3.3   The conclusion
Just as the introduction creates an impression, so the conclusion leaves an impression; and this is just as important. The purpose of a conclusion is to remind the reader of what you have achieved and accomplished in the course of the assignment. A conclusion is not a bland summary of what you have done – it is not a statement of your plan. It must:

1. state clearly your main idea, line of argument, or what strikes you as being the most important aspect of your answer

2. show how and why the argument or answer you have offered differs from, or qualifies, the assignment title.

Say how and why your answer relates to the title and to your statement of intent as set out in the introduction. Try to avoid being overcome by the sense of relief at finishing. You need to remind the reader of your discussion and draw the whole thing together. You should state briefly the conclusions of your argument. These need not be dramatic or Nobel Prize-winning. The conclusion should be accurate, supported by the main body of the text and clear. This will help the reader to grasp the argument in its totality.

1.4 Polishing

Effective communication is what makes good writers stand out. When you are writing essays, it is very easy to fall into the trap of thinking that this is between you and the page and you forget that a real person is going to have to read it and perhaps even enjoy it. Consider your reader.

Your reader is a well-informed academic who is going to take you and your essay seriously. The style is therefore formal. This does not mean that it has to be long-winded. It is very often the people who understand their subject best who can explain it most simply and directly. Those who have only half a grasp of what they are talking about are the ones who are most likely to dress up their shallow knowledge in dense language. They think they know what they want to say, but when it comes to putting it down on paper, the words won't come because they have not thought everything through. If you can say what you mean with absolute clarity, you will demonstrate your knowledge effectively. Look at every single sentence you write and ask yourself whether it is crystal clear. Trying to achieve this clarity will often expose a lack of understanding on your part and that is what makes essay writing such a good learning opportunity. You expose the gaps and work on them. Do not be tempted to fudge.

Remember Murphy's Law of Writing: if your readers can misunderstand something they will. (And Murphy was an optimist.)

1.5 Preparing for submission

A departmental stylesheet telling you how to set your work out is often given in a course handbook. If not, here are a few suggestions:

1. Make sure your typeface is big enough:

You could use 8 pt for footnotes at a pinch

but 10 pt is just about the limit that older eyes can read comfortably for any length of time.

12 pt is easy on the eye (especially for ageing academics who have a lot of essays to read).

2. A page with plenty of white space is more attractive than a black, solid block of text. Make sure you use big margins so that the marker can write helpful comments. Separate your paragraphs with a blank line instead of indenting.

3. You should indent the quotation if you are quoting more than one line of poetry, a hymn or a prayer, or more than three lines of prose. Note that when indentation is used for a quotation, there are no quotation marks.

4. Imaginative use of fonts may help to make a point but for the main body of your text avoid weird and wonderful fonts.

1.5.1 Footnotes or endnotes

Your departmental stylesheet may give a ruling on this. If not, try to do whatever helps the reader. It is an irritation constantly having to flick to the end of a text. On the other hand, too many footnotes on a page can make for a very ugly appearance. For a few short notes which are important to the understanding of the text, the foot of the page is best. If they are copious and more for form than necessity, tuck them away at the end.

1.5.2   *References and bibliographies*

The purpose of references and bibliographies is to enable your readers to find for themselves the material to which you have referred. They may want to check your accuracy or, more positively, they may be stimulated by your writing to go and find out more. Whenever you are picking up another author's idea, even if you are not using their exact words, it is usual to use the author's surname, the date of publication and the page number in brackets (Wiseman, 1999, p. 999 or Wiseman, 1999: 999) after the citation or, if the author's name is part of your text, just bracket the date and the page number: Wiseman (1999, p. 999) is a fictitious example. If an author has more than one publication of the same date, these are designated 1999a, 1999b, and so on, which will be listed in the bibliography at the end of the essay. Proper referencing is essential if you are not to be accused of plagiarism.

Plagiarism, whether intentional or unintentional, is a form of cheating which universities are very concerned about and they are increasingly vigilant to ensure that students do not copy work from other students, from published sources or from the Internet. There are even computer programs designed to detect plagiarism. Of course you will present and discuss other people's ideas, opinions and theories in your essay, but you must say where you found them and you must be very careful not to claim them as your own original thoughts.

Bibliographies are a horrible chore, but the task can be made a lot easier if you note all the necessary information right from the very beginning of your research. It is soul-destroying chasing round libraries looking for things like page numbers and place of publication when the rest of the job is done.

The perfectionist will ensure that the latest editions of books are consulted wherever possible but, if you cannot get hold of the most recent edition, list in your bibliography the one to which you referred.

If you are referring to a web site, you must make sure that you give enough information to make sure that a reader could access the same site. Give the date in case the site has been updated since you used it.

The exact formats for bibliographies vary greatly and attention should be paid to where full stops, commas and so on are
used. They are always in the alphabetical order of the authors'
surnames. If there is no set format, these are possible options:

Author, A. N. (1995) *Book Title in Italics*, Place: Publisher.

Author, A. N. (1996a) 'Article title without capitals,'
Italicised Journal Name, 10 (3): 1–55.

Author, A. N. (1996b) 'An essay in a book,' in S. Cribble
(ed.) *Book Title*, Place: Publisher.

1.6   Proof-reading

Always proof-read on a hard copy. You will need to proof-
read several times because you cannot do all the tasks at once.

Stage one

Take a break. It is very difficult to proof-read your own work
and the more of a distance you can put between writing and
re-reading the better.

Stage two

Read for general sense and good communication. Read it out
loud. Are there any bits that are unclear, get your tongue in a
twist or sound rather pompous? At this stage, do not stop to
correct things or you will lose the big picture. Just make a
mark in the margin. Have you got the balance right, spending
most time on the most important points? Once you have read
right through, wrestle with the awkward sentences. Be careful
that any improvements you make do not introduce new errors.
When you are sure you have done everything for your reader
that you would like an author to do for you, you may proceed
to the next stage.

Stage three

Do the mechanical bits in turn. Use the spellchecker but do
your own check for things that it will miss, like *it's/its*,
where/were. A very common kind of mistake is to mistype the

little words, *on* instead of *of* for example. Is your punctuation helpful? Work out all the sums, double check names and dates, physically look up everything that you have cross-referenced. When checking your grammar, common errors to look out for include verbs changing tense and pronouns drifting between *one* and *you*, sentences without verbs, run-on sentences where there should be a full stop in the middle, singular verbs with plural subjects and singular subjects with plural verbs.

Stage four

Give it to someone else to read, not necessarily a specialist in your subject. Ask them to make sure they can completely understand every sentence. In this way, they will test your own understanding. (Offer to do the same for them. You can learn a lot about your own writing from helping to make other people's writing clearer.)

Have a well-earned rest and look forward to an excellent mark. Then, when you get your essay back, resist the temptation to put it straight away in a file. Look at the comments carefully. If a few of you can get together and read each other's essays after marking, you get a much better understanding of what makes a good essay in your subject.

2. COMPLETE DISASTER

What do you do if, in spite of all the good advice in this book, you fail to hand your essay in on time? You may have a good reason, such as illness. If so, you should provide a medical certificate. Your director of studies or personal tutor should be notified of serious personal problems which interfere with your work and they may be taken into account if you find you need an extension. Having three essays to hand in for the same day does not constitute grounds for an extension. It is merely a fact of university life and a very good reason for organising your time wisely. As soon as you feel you are behind schedule, have a word with your tutor.

If the worst comes to the worst, face up to it. Go to your tutor, lecturer or course organiser, own up and apologise. The longer you leave it, the harder it will be. Do *not* try to explain how your hard disk ate your essay at the last moment: you should have kept a floppy copy. Nobody believes that computers crash two hours before the submission time. By that late hour you should have a copy already printed out for a final proof-read. You could hand that copy in if the computer crashes. Better to hand in a late draft than a draft late. You may find that you will be marked down for late submission but, if you have ignored all this advice, that is exactly what you deserve!

Essays are the most demanding pieces of writing that you will be asked to do in first year. In later years, you may be asked to do a much longer thesis or dissertation and you may even want to write papers for conferences or articles for publication. Essay writing trains you for these activities. The processes are just the same. If you keep the needs of your reader in mind, you will be able to write for all occasions.

2.1 Reminders of how to avoid disaster

- Make yourself comfortable in a distraction-free zone.

- Use mindmaps, flow charts and so on to help you your essay plan.

- Start writing as soon as you start researching.

- Try freewriting or talking to get started or to unblock you if you get stuck.

- Ask for help if you need it.

3. IMPROVING WRITTEN COMMUNICATION

As you progress through university, you will have to deal with more and more complex concepts and your teachers will demand ever more exacting standards of precision and accuracy. Such rigour in your thinking will be reflected in your writing style. Here are a few hints on how to achieve depth without sacrificing clarity in your academic writing.

3.1   Parts of paragraphs

3.1.1 Topic sentences
You should have one topic or core idea per paragraph. It is a good idea to summarise it in a topic sentence.

The best place for the topic sentence is at the beginning of the paragraph because it makes for easy reading if your reader knows what you are writing about. If your reader is scanning through your work, the first sentence of each paragraph will catch the eye. You can put it at the end, which is also a position which gives emphasis, but that makes it harder work for the reader. Of course, if you really want to drive a point home, you can put it at both beginning and end.

As you write, keep your topic sentence in mind. When you find yourself straying from it, you should be on to the next paragraph.

3.1.2   Conversation
When you are writing, you are holding a conversation without being able to hear the other person. At the end of each paragraph, in a conversation, your partner would come in with a comment like:

> *What happened next?*
> *Could you give me an example?*
> *You have given me a whole lot of examples. Are you going to infer something?*
> *Ah, but what if . . .?*
> *Are there any other ways of looking at this?*
> *Say that again another way. I didn't understand a word of it!*

If your paragraphs are well planned, your reader should be coming to the same conclusion as you, just milliseconds before you state what has just become obvious. Or, at least, they will be formulating the question which your next paragraph is just about to answer. If you have experienced this in your reading, you will know how good it makes a reader feel.

3.1.3 Linking

In the best writing, one paragraph naturally and necessarily flows on to the next. Between paragraphs, take time to reflect:

- What did I establish in the last paragraph?

- How does my next paragraph relate to it?

In case the relationship is not immediately clear, it is helpful to have a few strategies ready to help you link paragraphs to each other.

For example, you could start with a paragraph which lists the topics to be discussed in the following paragraphs. You could end with a paragraph that summarises the preceding paragraphs. That may not be appropriate if you are trying to follow an argument from beginning to end, in which case it might be helpful to have some signals ready to link paragraphs:

Enumerative:	*Firstly . . . Secondly . . . Finally . . .*
Additive:	*Another example . . . Furthermore . . . Moreover . . .*
Contrastive:	*By contrast . . . On the one hand . . . On the other hand . . . Alternatively . . .*

When you are reading, make a note of any links which you think are effective and which you would feel comfortable using.

Beware, however, of overusing any of these links as they can easily become intrusive and irritating. Watch your writing very carefully for links that are becoming too much of a habit; 'however' is frequently overused.

The length of paragraphs should be varied. A long paragraph is hard reading and it is good to put in short, signpost ones, just to say where you have got to or where you are going, if you think you might be overloading your reader. The more important the point, the longer the paragraph, but an occasional, very short, punchy paragraph can be used very effectively to hammer home a vital point.

3.2 Sentences

The important thing about sentences is to keep the words in the right order. Do not alter the natural word order for rhetorical effect unless you really know what you are doing and you are really sure that your meaning will be made more rather than less clear.

The subject of the sentence goes at the beginning. It is no accident that the grammatical 'subject', the one that 'does' the verb, goes before the verb. The subject is what the sentence is about and the rest of the sentence is saying something about the subject. The second most conspicuous position in a sentence is at the end. Occasionally, it can be effective to build up to a climax at the end of a sentence.

A sentence is as long as it needs to be. If you are building complex relationships, your sentence might have to be very long but, if you keep the structure simple, a long sentence does not have to be difficult. Do not try to tuck too many additional bits of information into a sentence or your reader will lose the main thread. Too many short sentences sound rather ugly and fail to develop links and relationships but the very occasional short, sharp sentence can give a dramatic emphasis. Try to give your reader a bit of variety in sentence length.

3.2.1 Be impersonal
Know when to take responsibility for your own actions and opinions. Departments, and even individual lecturers, vary in their acceptance of the use of *I* in academic writing, but there is an increasing awareness outside universities that the use of the passive is a way of avoiding responsibility. 'The report could not be submitted before the meeting' actually means

'Oops, I missed the deadline.' When you want to make it clear that you are voicing a purely personal opinion, *I* is not only appropriate but essential: *It might be thought that* . . . >I think . . . (Not: *The author thinks* . . .)

3.2.2 Be active

Using the passive is a way of avoiding the use of *I*, but there is so much of the passive in academic prose that it becomes wearisome. Therefore, avoid it if you can, for example, It has been suggested by Smith . . . > Smith has suggested . . .

3.2.3 Be positive

Negatives can overstretch your readers' logical abilities:

> *There are no conditions under which Buddhists will not use violence.*
> *The number of Hindus in India is not beyond eighty per cent of the total population*
> *Use of hallucinogenic drugs in shamanic rituals will not occur if insufficient numbers of shaman are not present.*

3.2.4 Be brief

Word limits take into account the number of words necessary to deal with the set topic. Using unnecessary words for padding out or running over the limit does not make a good essay or pleasant reading. By how much can you shorten these examples?

> *A feature of much of this research is the illustration of* . . .
> *There is continued, ongoing research* . . .
> *Basically, the true facts may be said to be as follows: an undue and excessive proliferation of redundant and unnecessary modifiers and other repetitious or fairly weak insertions add very little or nothing to the meaningful impact of the discourse.*

3.2.5 Be careful!

Sometimes you can be too brief:

> *Ritual circumcision is a way of life.*

Make sure that what goes together stays together:

Rabbit wanted for child with lop ears.

Sometimes you can say more than you intended:

The doctor said that he had never before seen this rare subcutaneous parasite in the flesh.

3.3 Vocabulary

3.3.1 Jargon
One person's technical term is another person's jargon. In choosing your words, keep your target reader constantly in mind. When you are writing for your tutors and lecturers, you should be able to show that you have understood the technical terms and can use them correctly and appropriately.

3.3.2 Big words
Do not use big words where little ones are adequate. If by *termination* you mean *end*, then use *end*. There is nothing to be gained by substituting *utilise* for *use*. There is a place for big words where they are the best ones to convey an accurate meaning, but they are not to be used unnecessarily for the sole purpose of sounding authoritative. You will just end up not knowing what you are talking about. Be especially self-disciplined about avoiding words whose meaning you are not completely sure about. Either consult a dictionary or use a word you know.

Re-write the following in plain English:
The noxious emissions from urban mobile sources are offensive to the olfactory organs.
(This can be reduced to three words: answer at the end of section 3)

3.3.3   Formality
You need to maintain a certain level of formality. In selecting short, commonly used words, you must avoid any slang terms and colloquialisms.

3.3.4   Premodifiers

The build-up of long, heavily premodified, fluency-impairing noun phrases is a common failing in academic writing.

This could be rephrased:

Too many adjectives before a noun often impair the fluency of academic writing.

3.3.5   More verbs
Verbs make your text bounce along. Nouns and adjectives and prepositional phrases describing nouns are solid and slow your reader down. If you can use more verbs and fewer adjectives and nouns, you will sound much less boring:

After expulsion of the breath by the lungs . . .
After the lungs expel the breath . . .

You can increase the proportion of verbs to nouns by rewriting phrases like

make an adjustment to > adjust
come to the conclusion > conclude

Other examples which can be shortened to a single verb include:

arrive at a decision
make an examination of
conduct an investigation into

3.4 Inference

In a real conversation, there is a lot of creativity coming from both sides. How many interpretations can you put on the following?

Where was I?
Are you on the phone?

These sentences work in conversation because you can rely on inference. You can give signals with your own facial expressions and other gestures. You alter your tone of voice. If an appropriate, unambiguous inference cannot be made, your hearer will ask what you mean. You can see if there is a blank or bewildered or angry or approving expression on a hearer's face. You can ask little 'tag' questions just to make sure the conversation is going as you intend. Right? When you write, you are deprived of all these safety checks.

You cannot assume that, just because your reader is an expert in the subject, he or she will know what you mean anyway and reconstruct some sense from your half-expressed musings.

3.5 Rhetoric

Figures of speech are more likely to be found in writing where the purpose is to persuade or entertain than in the dispassionate prose of academic discourse. They should be used sparingly, but there are a few good tricks which are useful for getting your point across.

3.5.1 Simile
If you are going to use similes, chose ones which are really vivid. If you describe a parasite as looking *like a courgette seed*, you need to be sure your readers are readily familiar with courgette seeds.

3.5.2   *Repetition*

Usually, you go to quite a lot of effort to vary your sentence structure. A deliberate repetition of a pattern can therefore attract and hold the reader's attention.

I came. I saw. I conquered.

Why do bears, wishes and Billy Goats Gruff always repetitively come in threes? The universality of the number three in folk-lore testifies to its power. Here is another triplet:

> *Some books are to be tasted, some to be swallowed whole and some few to be chewed and digested.* (Francis Bacon)

Here, the third time comes with a little extra. This is repetition and variation. Good writers have always exploited this device. Think of repetition with variation as the delivery of some weakening punches followed by the knock-out blow.

3.5.3   *Rhetorical question*

This can be very irritating if it is over-used. A useful strategy is to use a question as a topic sentence to open a paragraph, and then go on to answer it.

3.5.4   *Climax*

For maximum impact, make points in increasing order of importance so that the reader's interest grows to a peak. If you do it the other way round, the reader will be bored by mid-sentence. Similarly, always give your weakest examples or weakest arguments first and save the best for last.

3.6   Professional spelling

Spelling mistakes create a bad impression especially when you make mistakes with technical terms specific to your subject; you undermine your readers' faith in your professional ability. Use your spellchecker to teach yourself spelling. If a word keeps coming up, take a moment to learn it. The academic writer always has a good dictionary and a glossary of technical terms in the study of religions to hand and uses them.

3.7 Punctuation

Punctuation is not there for decoration but to help the reader. Too much punctuation can get in the way of fluent reading and if you put a piece of punctuation in the wrong place, it is obvious that you do not know what you are doing, whereas if you leave a piece of punctuation out it looks like a typing error. The lazy student will therefore follow the maxim: when in doubt, leave it out, and even the skilful student will use punctuation economically.

3.7.1 Full stops
Between the capital letter and the full stop there should be one, and only one, complete statement.

3.7.2 Commas
Commas separate lists. Note that there is no comma before the *and* in British English.

> *The colours of the rainbow are red, orange, yellow, green, blue, indigo and violet.*

Commas separate out non-essential bits (essential in upper case):

> *Suddenly, THE DOOR SLAMMED.*
> *Because the door slammed, THE MAID SCREAMED.*
> *Meanwhile, back at the ranch, TONTO WAS, with great skill, MAKING PANCAKES.*

Note how commas can change meaning. Compare

> *The chainsaw jugglers, who had been drinking before the show, beheaded themselves.*

with

> *The chainsaw jugglers who had been drinking before the show
> beheaded themselves.*

In the first sentence, the bit in commas is an optional extra and
all the jugglers in the sentence lost their heads. In the second
sentence, the beheaded jugglers are limited to those who had
been drinking. Think about the effect of adding commas to:

> *The students who are good at punctuation do well in their essays.*

If a section in commas is, as here, in the middle of the sentence, make sure your commas come in pairs.

3.7.3   Brackets
They come in pairs too.

3.7.4   Dashes
Dashes can be used in much the same way as commas and
brackets, for sectioning off an optional extra but they should
not be used to hang afterthoughts on to the end of sentences.
  Brackets and dashes can be useful if commas start nesting.
Compare

> *Bad writers, who frequently compose long-winded sentences,
> rendered, as this example shows, incomprehensible, more or less,
> to the average or even skilled reader, by the interpolation of little,
> badly positioned, extra bits, should be ostracised by the academic
> community.*

with

> *Bad writers (who frequently compose long-winded sentences,
> rendered – as this example shows – incomprehensible to the
> average, or even skilled reader, by the interpolation of little, badly
> positioned, extra bits) should be ostracised by the academic
> community.*

The second version is still dreadful, but not quite so night-marish as the first.

3.7.5   Semicolons

If you feel that two sentences are so closely linked that you want to draw attention to the fact, you can use a semicolon instead of a full stop:

> *The students got very high marks; nothing in their answers was irrelevant to the question.*

Semicolons are also useful for lists where the items consist of more than one word, especially if the individual items contain commas:

> *I shared a flat with three exotic dancers from a Paris nightclub; a large, brown rat, who snored; a highly intelligent, but eccentric, philosophy student, called Alfie, who had a pet snake called Lucy; an ex-politician; and several cockroaches.*

3.7.6   Colons

You will notice how colons are used to introduce lists and examples in this book. They are also used to introduce quota-tions when no verb of saying is present.

3.7.7   Exclamation marks

Avoid them! They have very little place in academic discourse. And never, never, *never* use more than one at a time.

3.7.8   Hyphens

These can be useful for resolving ambiguities. Consider the difference between

> *extra-marital sex* and *extra marital sex.*

Hyphens should also be used to avoid weird spellings: *de-ice* rather than *deice* and *go-between* rather than *gobetween*.

If you are not sure whether a compound word is hyphenated or not, and you cannot find it in your dictionary, make a decision and stick to it.

3.7.9 Quotation marks

Use quotation marks for short quotes but do not use them for 'iffy' words. If you think a word is not quite consistent with your formality level, find an 'un-iffy' word instead.

3.7.10 Apostrophes

Apostrophes are the punctuation marks that people seem to find hardest. In fact, they are really easy. In very formal writing, you will not use apostrophes for shortened words. *Do not write don't. It's it is, isn't it?*

> Apostrophes are used to show possession.
> If the possessor is singular, use apostrophe s (*the queen's crown*)
> If the possessor is plural and ends in -s, use s apostrophe (*cats' tails*)
> If the possessor is plural and does not end in -s, use apostrophe s (*men's heads*)
> In other words, make the plural first and the possessive second.

Special care is needed with personal names ending in -s like *William James* and *Moses* or *Hinnells*. There is a convention which allows these names just to have an apostrophe: *James' philosophy*, although *James's* possessive form may also be made safely in the usual way by adding 's after the complete surname. It is a common mistake to put the apostrophe inside the name: *Hinnells' books* are very popular, but *Hinnell's books* have been written by the less well-known Mr Hinnell.

If the possessor is a pronoun, do not use an apostrophe. You would never dream of writing *hi's*, would you? The same goes for *its. His head. Its tail.*

This is not all that there is to say about punctuation, but it might be enough to prevent the commonest errors. When checking your punctuation, the question to ask yourself is always: 'Does it help the reader?'

3.8   Answer to big-words exercise

City traffic stinks.

4.   WRITING SKILLS SELF-ASSESSMENT

When you have completed a piece of work, check it on the table below. Note down your strengths and weaknesses. Now and again when you write, look back on the comments on your earlier work. Have you taken your own and tutors' criticisms on board?

CONSTRUCTIVE COMMENTS

First impression:
Layout
Word-processing
Attention to detail

Paragraphs:
Length
Signposting
Conversation
Linking

Sentences:
Length
Clarity
Grammar

Vocabulary:
Consistent formality
Accuracy
Clarity

Spelling:

Punctuation:
Accuracy
Helpfulness

Other comments:

GLOSSARY

Adi Granth Literally 'first book', the scriptures of Sikhism, also known as The Guru Granth Sahib.

Advaita Vedanta One of the three divisions of Vedanta, which is one of the six orthodox viewpoints, or schools of Hinduism.

Allah The Arabic term for God.

Amrit The 'nectar of immortality' used as an image and the sweetened baptismal water taken by Sikhs during initiation.

Anglican Another term for the Church of England, which separated itself from the authority of Rome in the sixteenth century under Henry VIII.

Animism The belief that there is spirit or life in everything.

Aryan Migrants to northern India about 4,000 years ago. Used to mean 'noble' in Buddhism. Mis-used by Nazis.

Atman Hindu term for eternal self or soul.

Atonement The Christian teaching that through the incarnation and sacrificial death of Jesus on the cross humans can once more enter into a right relationship, and be at one, with God.

Avatar A Hindu concept of the 'descent' or manifestation of a deity, especially of Vishnu. Famous avatars are Krishna and Rama.

Bahai Religion founded in Iran by Baha'u'llah in the 1860s and now world-wide.

Baptism Literally 'washing'. Ritual washing is practised in many faiths but this term ususally applies to a Christian rite of initiation either of children or adults.

Baptist The name of a group of Protestant Christian churches which believe that adults undergo baptism by immersion as a sign of faith.

Bhagavad Gita The Song of The Lord (see Mahabharata).

Bhagavata Purana (see Krishna).

Bhakti Loving devotion to a deity in Hinduism.

Bible Literally 'book' or 'books', usually the Christian scriptures, made up of Old and New Testaments. Testament is the Latin word for covenant or agreement and the books of the covenant with the Jewish people are called the Old Testament by Christians (see Tenakh).

Brahma Kumaris A spiritual movement founded in India in 1937 CE and led mainly by women. Now world-wide.

Brahman Transpersonal Ultimate Reality in Hinduism.

Brahmin Hindu priest (see varna).

Buddha Title meaning an enlightened or awakened one.

Calligraphy The art of beautiful writing.

Chetuvim Also Ketubim (see Tenakh).

Christ Literally 'annointed one', from a Greek equivalent of the Hebrew term 'Messiah'.

Church The Christian community which gives its name to the building where Christians meet for worship.

Cosmological Argument An attempt to prove the existence of God from the existence of the universe.

Cult A term for a non-traditional religious movement or ritual.

Culture The whole way of life of a group or society.

Daoism Also Taoism. Chinese religious and philosophical system based on the teachings of Lao-tzu and the Dao-te ching about the 'Way'.

Darshan Sanskrit for 'viewing' the deity or a holy person. The term 'darshana' (viewpoint) is used for six orthodox schools of thought in Hinduism.

Dharma A wide Sanskrit term which can be translated as 'truth', 'teaching', 'righteousness' or 'duty'. Hindus have suggested that 'sanatana dharma' is a better term for their traditions than Hinduism.

Diaspora Originally the dispersed Jewish communities, but now used for all dispersed, transnational groups.

Eastern Orthodox (see orthodox).

Eidetic Vision Capacity to see the essentials or essence.

Emic The insiders' understanding.

Enlightenment This term might be used in two ways. It can refer to the attainment of insight and wisdom (see Buddha). It is also used to refer to the eighteenth-century European cultural and intellectual movement. This is also called 'the age of reason' because individuals began to challenge external authority and dogma. The Jewish term is 'Haskalah'.

Epistemology Reflection on how knowledge arises.

Epoché Distancing oneself or suspending one's value judgements when studying a tradition.

Ethnography In-depth studies of individuals and communities based on attentive listening and observation which may challenge generalisations.

Etic The observer or outsider's viewpoint.

Feminist/feminism Viewpoint which gives priority to women's perspectives.

Goddess The divine in a female form.

Golden temple (see Harimandir).

Gospel Literally 'good news'. The name given to four perspectives on the story of Jesus named Matthew, Mark, Luke and John.

Granthi A Sikh man or woman who reads from the Guru Granth Sahib during worship.

Gurdwara Wherever the Guru Granth Sahib is installed, which becomes a Sikh place of worship.

Guru Spiritual teacher in Hinduism. Sikh term for God, who is Waheguru (Wonderful Lord) and for the ten historical leaders of the community and the scriptures.

Guru Granth Sahib (see Adi Granth).

Hadith Sayings and practices of Muhammad (see also sunna(h)). After the *Qur'an* the second source of authority for Muslims.

Hajj Muslim pilgrimage to Makka, one of the five pillars and obligatory once in a lifetime.

Hare Krishna (see ISKCON).

Harimandir A building constructed at Amritsar in which the fifth Sikh Guru Arjan installed the Adi Granth. Also called the Golden Temple.

Hermeneutics Principles of interpretation.

Holography A holographic image is a picture of a totality the parts of which also show the whole.

Humanism Beliefs and values that are not rooted in religion.

Indigenous The preferred term for the original religions of a particular locality.

Injil The Arabic word for 'gospel', Allah's teaching through Jesus.

Insider A member of a group or tradition.

ISKCON The International Society for Krishna Consciousness, a Hindu movement whose central practice imitates Chaitanya (1485–1533 CE), who danced and sang the names of God (Hari Krishna, Hari Rama) in the streets.

Istadevata The deity a Hindu chooses for his or her personal devotion.

Jains An ancient Indian religion of renunciates supported by householders which is based on the teachings of twenty-four jinas (spiritual victors), the twenty-fourth of which, Mahavira, lived at the same time as Gautama Buddha.

Jehovah's Witnesses A Christian-derived movement from the end of the nineteenth century which is literal in its interpretation of the Bible and emphasises the imminent coming of God's kingdom.

Jnana A Sanskrit term for spiritual knowledge.

Kabbala(h) Jewish mystical teachings.

Karma Literally 'action'. A Hindu, Buddhist and Sikh idea that there is a law that what you sow, you will reap, in Buddhism based on intention.

Ketuvim Also Chetubim, the third section of the Jewish scriptures (see tenakh).

Khalifa(h) Viceregent or trustee responsible to Allah. Used for human responsibility in the world and a term for a ruler, anglicised as caliph.

Khalsa Sikh community of those who have become initiated and wear the five 'Ks': uncut hair (*kesh*), which is kept clean with a comb (*kangha*); a sword (*kirpan*); shorts (*kach*) usually as an undergarment, and wristlet (*kara*).

Kirtan The singing of hymns from the Sikh scriptures.

Krishna An avatar of Vishnu about whom cycles of stories are found in the Bhagavad Gita and Bhagavata Purana.

Lama Tibetan term for a spiritual teacher or guru.

Langar The free meal served to anyone visiting a gurdwara and the area where the meal is served.

Legend Story based on, but expanding, historical fact.

Madrasa(h) Islamic place of education for children or adults.

Magic Words or actions drawing on supernatural power which produce an effect.

Mahabharata A great Indian epic which developed over a long period of time and which contains the Bhagavad Gita, probably the most popular, though not the most sacred, Hindu scripture focusing on Krishna's teaching to Arjuna.

Mahayana Literally 'great way' and a collective name for those Buddhist ideas and movements which initially spread north and east from India, but have now also come West. They include the Zen, Pure Land and Tibetan schools.

Maori Indigenous peoples of the Pacific, particularly New Zealand.

Methodist An eighteenth-century movement, based on strict methods of spiritual practice. At first within the Church of England, it was begun by John and Charles Wesley and others and became a separate Christian denomination.

Moksha Liberation from samsara in Hinduism.

Monotheism Belief in One God.

Moonie (see Unification Church).

Mormon A Christian-derived movement also called the Church of Jesus Christ of The Latter Day Saints whose members believe that *The Book of Mormon* was revealed to Joseph Smith in 1822.

Mosque A Muslim place of prostration or prayer.

Myth A story which conveys a deep spiritual meaning or truth.

Neviim The Prophetic section of the Jewish scriptures (see Tenakh).

New Testament (see Bible).

Nirvana The Sanskrit term used particularly in Buddhism for the state when the fires of greed, hatred and ignorance are extinguished.

Numinous Something mysterious which is awe-inspiring and attractive.

Old Testament (see Bible).

Omnipotent All-powerful.

Omniscient All-knowing.

Ontological Argument Attempt to prove the existence of God as 'a being than whom no greater can be conceived'.

Orthodox In general this means 'right belief'. It is also a term used for particular movements in both Judaism and Christianity. Orthodox and Ultra-Orthodox Jews believe in the divinely-given inerrancy of the Torah and their obligation to live by its teachings. Eastern Orthodox Christians in Greece, Russia, Romania and so on claim to be the earliest form of Christianity and still use a fourth-century form of service.

Orthopraxy Right practice.

Outsider A person who is not a member of a group or tradition.

Pagan/paganism A term used for the religious traditions that Christians rejected, but now used positively for the original, indigenous spiritual traditions of Europe.

Pali Canon The sacred scriptures of Theravada Buddhists in the Pali language (also called Tripitaka, three baskets). They were collected into three parts, the Vinaya, Sutta and Abhidhamma Pitakas, and written on palm leaves.

Patriarchy The male (literally 'father') as normative and dominant in language and power relationships.

Pentecostals Groups of Christians who receive as a gift of the Holy Spirit speaking in tongues like the early Christians on the day of Pentecost in the book of Acts Chapter 2.

Pesach The Jewish feast of Passover which commemorates the liberation of the Hebrew slaves from Egypt. In Jewish homes an order of service (seder) uses specific foods and the questions of children to tell the story of the Exodus.

Polytheism Belief in many gods.

Pope Literally 'father', came to be used for the Bishop of Rome who is seen as the leading authority of the Roman Catholic Church.

Primitive A term used by early anthropologists for the religious beliefs and practices of tribal or indigenous peoples.

Projection The suggestion that what is only a human idea, value or relationship is Divine and of ultimate worth, for example that God is our Father.

Protestant Christian movements rooted in the sixteenth-century Reformation which protested against the beliefs and practices of the Roman Catholic Church and protested a Biblical faith based on grace. These now include Lutherans, Calvinists, Baptists, Presbyterians and many others.

Purim A Jewish festival which celebrates Esther and Mordecai's plan to save the Jewish people from Haman's plot to kill them.

Quaker (see Society of Friends).

Qualitative Research methods based on interviews and participant observation.

Quantitative Research methods based on the analysis of numerical data.

Qur'an Arabic for 'recitation'. The Holy Book of Islam.

Rabbi A Jewish teacher or scholar and now the leader of a congregation.

Ramakrishna Vedanta Mission A Hindu movement based on the teachings of Ramakrishna (1836–86 CE) and brought to the West by Vivekananda.

Ramayana An Indian epic which tells the story of Rama and Sita.

Reductionist/reductive Suggesting that talking about God or the divine is no more than talking about human ideas and relationships.

Reform Judaism Movement established in the nineteenth century which uses vernacular languages instead of Hebrew in services, allows women rabbis and has a more liberal interpretation of Torah than the Orthodox.

Reformation (see Protestant).

Roman Catholic Originally the Western church, but now world-wide with its headquarters in Rome. It parted from the Eastern Orthodox churches in 1054 CE and Protestant groups broke away in the sixteenth century.

Rosh Hashanah The Jewish New Year in the autumn.

Sampradaya Term for a Hindu movement.

Samsara The cycle of birth, death and rebirth from which Hindus, Buddhists and Sikhs differently seek release.

Sanatana Dharma (see Dharma).

Sangha Buddhist community of monks, nuns, laymen and lay-women, often used simply for monastics.

Satori A term in Zen Buddhism for sudden enlightenment.

Science(s) A variety of ways of studying and knowing which are based on observation, experimentation, inductive reasoning, collecting, classifying and comparing data.

Sect Minority religious group. The term is often used critically.

Secular/secularisation Not distinctively religious or sacred.

Seder (see Pesach).

Shar'ia(h) Islamic system of law, literally 'the path to water', which is the source of life.

Shi'a Short for 'Shiat Ali', the Party of Ali, who in various sub-groups make up 12–15 per cent of Muslims.

Shoah Literally 'catastrophe', 'desolation' or 'destruction', this is the Jewish term for the murder of six million Jews by the Nazis during World War II. Also called the Holocaust.

Society of Friends A Christian movement deriving from the preaching of George Fox in the seventeenth century. It emphasises silent worship except when a person is spiritually moved (quakes) to speak. Strong commitment to non-violence and equality of persons, all of whom have an inner light.

Soka Gakkai A new Japanese Buddhist movement for the creation of values based on the teachings of Nichiren (1222–82 CE) and founded in the 1930s. The focus of practice is the chanting of the name of the Lotus Sutra, 'Nam Myoho Renge Kyo'.

Spirituality A term which evokes an inner, personal experience of meaning either within or apart from religious institutions.

Sufi Muslim term for mystic.

Sukkot The Jewish autumn festival of tabernacles which remembers the 40 years living in tents in the wilderness in the time of Moses.

Sunna(h) The collection of traditions of Muhammad's words and deeds (see Hadith).

Sunni The term for the majority (about 85 per cent) of Muslims who claim to follow the sunna(h) or traditions of the prophet, as distinct from *Shi'a* Muslims.

Sunyata (Sanskrit) Emptiness. One of many terms used in Buddhism (see Nirvana) for ultimate reality when the impermanent features of conventional reality are removed.

Swaminarayan A Hindu movement founded in the nineteenth century by Sahajananda who is considered an avatar of Vishnu. Spread to the UK in the 1950s and opened Neasden Temple in 1995.

Synagogue Jewish meeting place for reading and debating Torah and for worship.

Talmud The collection of the discussions of over a thousand Jewish rabbis over many centuries. It includes the Mishna(h) and has a Babylonian and Jerusalem version, the former, which dates from about 600 CE, being the more authoritative.

Tenakh (also Tanach) The acronym for the books of the Jewish scriptures standing for Torah (teaching or law), Neviim (prophets) and Ketuvim (writings).

Theodicy The problem of God's justice in the face of the existence of evil and suffering in the world.

Theravada The way of the elders; the name for the surviving school of southern or Pali Buddhism found classically in Sri Lanka, Thailand, Myanmar and Campuchea and now also in the West.

Torah Teaching, the name given to the first five books of the Jewish scriptures, which are also called the Law (see Tenakh).

Totem An animal, plant or other object with which a social group identifies.

Umma(h) The Muslim term for community or the people of Muhammad.

Unification Church A Christian-derived movement founded by the Korean Sun Myung Moon (b. 1920) who is seen as the spiritual leader of the age. Also known as Moonies.

Unitarian A Christian-derived movement which began in the UK and the USA in the eighteenth century. Distinctive beliefs are the unity of Divine Reality and that spirituality is rooted in experience.

Upanishad A body of Hindu scriptures which explore the unity of the individual atman with Brahman.

Valmiki The legendary author of the Ramayana. A Punjabi movement (also called Balmikis) has grown up which reveres him and both the Hindu Ramayana and Sikh Adi Granth.

Varna The social hierarchy (class or caste) of classical Hinduism, consisting of Brahmins (priests); Kshatryas (rulers and warriors); Vaishyas (artisans and traders); Shudras (serfs) and those who are outside the system (outcastes or dalits).

Veda Literally 'knowledge'. The name given to the most authoritative collection of Hindu scriptures which includes the four Samhitas, Brahmanas, Aranyakas and Upanishads.

Verstehen An act of understanding involving empathy.

Yeshiva(h) A centre of advanced Jewish study.

Yoga Physical and meditational disciplines or exercises which can lead to liberation in Hinduism. It is also the name given to one of the six orthodox schools of Hindu philosophy and to a collection of sutras.

Yom Kippur The Jewish Day of Atonement.

INDEX

A Companion to Religious Studies and Theology

Edited by HELEN K. BOND, SETH D. KUNIN and FRANCESCA ARAN MURPHY

This *Companion* offers a comprehensive introduction to the subject areas of both Religious Studies and Theology, covering Judaism, Christianity, Islam, Hinduism, Buddhism, New Religious Movements, Practical Theology, Systematic Theology, The Bible, Philosophy of Religion, Psychological, Anthropological and Sociological theories, all in one inclusive volume.

Based on the core components of Religious Studies and Theology degrees, it is designed to function as the main text for beginning students, and for use throughout their studies. Stimulating and broad-ranging, it is divided into two parts – Religious Studies and Theology – and six main sections:

- Religious Studies
- Case Studies: World Religions
- Biblical Studies
- Systematic Theology
- Theories of Religion
- Theology
- Practical Theology
- The Philosophy of Religion.

This blend of perspectives offers a balanced overview of the field a whole.

Key Features:
- A one-stop bumper textbook for Religious Studies and Theology students
- Comprehensive coverage of all aspects of the subject
- Key terms defined and highlighted
- Questions at the end of each chapter
- Guides to further reading

Contents:
Introduction

Part 1: Religious Studies
Section 1: Theories of Religion 1. The Theology of Religion (Douglas Davies) 2. Psychological and Phenomenological Theories of Religion (Seth D. Kunin) 3. Anthropological and Sociological Theories of Religion (Seth D. Kunin)
Section 2: Case Studies 1. Indigenous Traditions and Anthropological Theory (Seth D. Kunin) 2. Judaism (Seth D. Kunin) 3. Christianity (Douglas Davies) 4. Islam (Hugh Goddard) 5. Hinduism and Buddhism (Martin Mills) 6. New Religious Movements and the New Age (Matthew Wood) 7. Recent Trends in Religion (Michael Perko)

Part 2: Theology
Section 3: Biblical Studies 1. Ways of Reading the Bible (Paul Ellingworth) 2. Introduction to the Hebrew Bible (Ken Aitken) 3. Introduction to the New Testament (Helen K. Bond)
Section 4: Practical Theology 1. What is Practical Theology (John Swinton)
Section 5: Systematic Theology 1. An Overview of Christian History (Henry Sefton) 2. Christology from the Apostolic Age to Chalcedon (Francesca Aran Murphy) 3. The Bases of Systematic Theology (Francesca Aran Murphy) 4. The Holy Spirit, Creeds and the Church (Francesca Aran Murphy) 5. Revelation and the Trinity (Francesca Aran Murphy)
Section 6: Philosophy of Religion 1. The Philosophy of Religion (Derek Cross)

April 2003 • 640pp • Paperback 0 7486 1457 5 • Hardback 0 7486 1456 7